Within Her Grasp

Joanne Simon Tailele

Jacobs Writing Consultants, LLC

Contributions by Marion Kminek

Copyright © June2015

First Edition

Disclaimer and Acknowledgments

This is the story of Mari-Rae Sopper

June 19, 1966 – September 11, 2001

As much as the author has attempted to be accurate, some poetic license has been incorporated to capture life the way Mari-Rae might have reflected on it or experienced it first-hand. Most of the dialogue and internal thoughts are the product of the author's imagination. Dozens of family and friends candidly told of their experiences with Mari-Rae. Many of the lines in this book are direct quotes from her family and friends. For the sake of continuity in the story, each is not recognized as such. Please know that your contributions are greatly appreciated.

Contributions have been supplied in alphabetical order: Jim Bailey, Jennifer Rudy Bannon, Susan Blake, Mark Diab, Courtney Jackson Duncan, Jennifer Eichenmeuller, Kathy Edwards Federico, Conn Flanigan, Lindy Franzini-Carpenter, Debbie Diskerud Hatanpa, Annie Hernandez, Dawn Testo Hichew, Captain Sandra Jamison Hodgkinson, Ennis Hudson, Mike Jacki, Deb Bryant Janssen, Christina Kminek, Frank Kminek, Sr., Marion Kminek, Carmen Kruger, Sandra Oldham, Larry Petrillo, Mike Sharples, Denise Shipley, Julie Soldat Sullivan, Lynn Sopper, Barb Tsutsumi. If there have been any omissions, please accept our sincere apologies. Your contributions are greatly appreciated.

Research materials used in the formation of this book obtained from American Airlines, 9/11 Commission, JAG, USA Gymnastics, Iowa State Cyclone Gymnastics, Nadia Comãneci, Chalked Up by Jennifer Sey, The Unquiet Mind by Kay Redfield Jamison.

A few people asked for their names to be changed for privacy. We respected their wishes.

Impossible Dream

To dream the impossible dream
To fight the unbeatable foe
To bear with unbearable sorrow
To run where the brave dare not go
To right the unrightable wrong
To love pure and chaste from afar
To try when your arms are too weary
To reach the unreachable star
This is my quest
To follow that star
No matter how hopeless
No matter how far
To fight for the right
Without question or pause
To be willing to march into Hell
For a heavenly cause
And I know if I'll only be true
To this glorious quest
That my heart will lie peaceful and calm
When I'm laid to my rest
And the world will be better for this
That one man, scorned and covered with scars
Still strove with his last ounce of courage
To reach the unreachable star

Composed by Mitch Leigh
Jan. 30, 1928 – March 16, 2014

Lyrics written by Joe Darion
Jan 30, 1922 – June 6, 2001

Table of Contents

Prologue

Mari-Rae didn't need an alarm or coffee to be up and peeking out of her friend's upscale D.C. condo before dawn on this beautiful Tuesday Indian summer day. Not just up, but practically vibrating excitement. It was here. Now! The beginning of a new life, *the life* she had dreamed about since she was ten years old. She paused for a moment in the pre-dawn hour and remembered how it all began.

The year was 1976 and she was ten-years-old. On the small television in her family room, Nadia Comãneci scored a perfect ten on the uneven bars. It was the Summer Olympics in Montreal. She vowed that someday she, Mari-Rae Sopper, would be a professional gymnast. That vision of Nadia, as sharp and vivid as when she first saw it, had been set on auto-play in her mind every day since, taunting her to make her dream come true. And now, it was.

Her new job as head women's gymnastics coach at the University of California Santa Barbara was waiting for her. Never mind that she was taking a seventy percent cut in pay from her current position as a D.C. attorney. Never mind that they said it was only a one-year position and the program was being cut at the end of that year. That's what they thought. She had a plan. She *always* had a plan. For UCSB, there would be fund raisers, alumni and booster participation, and a lot of publicity. She would save the program. It was a given. Anyone who knew Mari-Rae would agree.

She left a voice message for her friend, Jim Bailey, that she'd be ready in half an hour. Should she give a last call to her mother? No, she was probably getting ready to head out for a real estate listing appointment. One of the many things Mari-Rae had learned from her mother was perseverance.

She ran down the stairs to her own empty condo. She stepped through the door, a jumble of emotions fluttering her rapidly beating heart: sadness over leaving so many wonderful friends, jubilation about her new position.

"Seriously, Sammy?" She pinched her nose. The hardwood floors were peppered with piles of watery cat feces. "What was wrong with your litter box?" Ah, it was full, too. The medication from the vet was supposed to calm him down for the flight. Wrong. And they never mentioned this unsavory side-effect.

Her feline companion responded by a leap straight into the air from his perch on the spiral staircase, a virtual orange and white striped rocket, that took off across the empty room at a speed that would have made Coach Petrillo proud. Then he slid into the wall—*thud!*

Mari-Rae laughed and shook her head. "Better get your running out of your system now. You'll be stuck in that carrier on the plane for several hours."

Things to do rushed through her head. Shower, check. Light make-up, check. She donned a simple A-line skirt and a button down sweater. It was always chilly on planes and she was always cold. She surveyed herself in the mirror. An even hundred brush strokes. Her dark blond hair shone like the smile on her face. She slipped on a pair of simple flats; easier to maneuver through the airport concourse.

Did she have all the information on the team in her bag? Check. She'd go over them again on the flight. Not that she didn't already know every team member by name, their statistics and where they excelled. She had always had the uncanny ability to remember names, scores and details like a flash drive in her head. Ryann was going to be great on beam. Erika only needed some good choreography to win competitions on floor. She loved each and every one of them already.

Jim arrived on time. He beeped the horn. *How did she always manage to get me to drive her to the airport?* Next time he would tell her, "Us city-folk take a taxi." He waited thirty minutes and finally let himself into her condo. Mari-Rae was still running around, ass on fire. What else was new?

He lifted her red backpack to carry to his car. "Ugh," he groaned. "What do you have in here, rocks?" If it made it on as a carry-on, it would be a miracle.

"What?" Mari-Rae looked up from her hands and knees on the hardwood floor. "That's my purse. Can you give me a hand here?" Mari-Rae waved a frantic hand toward the paper towels.

"If I weren't such a good friend…." Jim started as he knelt over a pile, his nose wrinkled from the God-awful smell.

"I know, I know," said Mari Rae as she finished up. "What do you think, Sammy? Are you ready?"

The ride through the Virginia countryside to Dulles Airport was beautiful. If Mari-Rae noticed it, she didn't say. The sun was rising behind the Washington Monument as they crossed the Potomac River merging on to Rt. 66. For forty minutes, she expounded on the qualities of her new team, how she was going to save the program. This time, this move, would be perfect. Her dream was finally in her grasp.

Jim dropped her off at the curb for departing flights to American Airlines. She hoisted the red backpack over the shoulder of her five-foot-two frame as he unloaded the rest of her luggage and the kitty crate. Life was going to be different without Jim around. She'd miss him. Of course there was still email and phone. They'd talk all the time, she assured herself. They hugged.

"Oh, I don't have any ones. Help me out?" she laughed. *So, shoot me,* she thought. Small details like that didn't make it into her computer brain. They didn't register high on the "needs" list.

Jim shook his head, dug into his wallet, and handed over his only ones to tip the luggage handler. "Call me when you get to Santa Barbara," he said.

Of course. He was one of her closest friends.

She waved as he honked and drove away. She looked up at the perfectly blue sky, not a cloud in site. Whew. This was it. Her new life. She remembered the title of the last group email she had sent to all of her family and friends, *New Job, New City, New State, New Life.* If joy was a drink, hers would be an orange Fizzy, like the sugary tablet she dropped into water as a child.

At airport security, she let Sammy out to get some air before the flight and placed the kitty crate on the conveyor belt to go through the scanner. He clung to her like an infant on his mother's shoulder, digging his back claws into her chest. Her eyes began to water from too much fur close to her face. Did she remember her allergy medicine? Yes, of course.

Okay. So maybe letting Sammy out of the cage wasn't one of her best decisions.

She started to walk through the scanner with Sammy on her shoulder.

"Ma'am," a security guard stopped her. "You'll have to put the cat in the carrier, while it goes through the scanner.

Getting him back into the carrier was a war of the wills. Once she pried him from her shoulder, his paws clung to the outside of the cage door, spread-eagled, Felix-the-Cat like. Two security guards had to assist in winning over Sammy's determination to stay out of that crate. She made her way back to the front of the line and walked through the scanner alone.

Two Middle-Eastern men stood stoically behind her in line. She glanced up at them and profusely apologized for Sammy's rude behavior. They nodded without speaking.

The alarms went off. Mari-Rae and the two gentlemen behind her were pulled aside where the security guard waved a wand over them and finally allowed them to go to the gate. The rest of the passengers went straight through.

All cleared, she picked up her backpack and Sammy in the carrier, and asked for directions to the gate. The two Middle-Eastern gentlemen followed her to the same gate.

Finally, at 7:50 a.m., she was settled in her seat, American Airlines Flight 77, Dulles International to LAX, Los Angeles, California. Her seatbelt was on. The stack of papers about "her girls" tucked in the magazine compartment in front of her waiting for her review. Mari-Rae looked around at the half-empty plane. Her aisle seat was perfect for introducing herself to the fellow passengers across the aisle and in the seat next to hers. "Where are you headed? Wasn't life wonderful?"

Within Her Grasp

1 Early Childhood - Spit and Vinegar

*"She was a strong child, which I considered to be a
positive quality and one of her strengths."
Mrs. Barbara Tsutsumi, First Grade Teacher,
Hunting Ridge School*

Five-pound-half-ounce Mari-Rae Sopper was
born on Father's Day, June 19, 1966, two weeks late, to
Marion and Bill Sopper of Hoffman Estates, Illinois. Her
mother would say she was bull-headed from the day she
was born. Once, as an infant, she held her breath while
crying when her diaper was being changed and passed
out. Grandma Dahlstrom from the farm in Elgin would
have said she was "willful, full of spit and vinegar."
Sister, Lynn, born two years after Mari-Rae, might have
used the term "spoiled" once or twice. But it wasn't
because they ever had a lot. Like any middle-class
American family, they struggled to make ends meet. The
one thing Mari-Rae had that stood out from everyone
else was determination. When Mari-Rae set her mind to
something, there was no stopping her.

Evenings were never a pleasant time for infant
Mari-Rae, and she screamed non-stop from six to ten
p.m. Whether it was colic or something else, in the '60s,

parents simply accepted it as normal. Finally, Marion added cereal to her bottle with a wide nipple before bedtime, and thankfully, Mari-Rae slept through the night.

Perhaps she was born to be a gymnast because Mari-Rae never crawled. That took too long. She could roll her way around a room much faster. Her first floor routine? At around one year old, she stood up and walked. And never stopped moving from that moment on. Walking merged into running and running into climbing. She climbed on everything. She'd climb out of her crib and, ready to get the day going, run to the highchair, climb in, and pound on the tray until Mom showed up to feed her.

Typical of most little girls, Mari-Rae loved her dolls and kissed and put them to bed like any good Mommy-to-be. And Mommy had to have a Daddy, as evidenced by family home videos showing the precocious little Mari-Rae planting her fist kiss on a boy before her second birthday. She loved her Daddy. She'd sit at the top of the steps waiting for Daddy to come home from work and slid down the stairs on her bottom to meet him at the door. He'd pick her up and spin her around. They had a special bond that would last through her entire life.

At about two-and-a-half years old, before secure car seats and automatic lock windows, Mari-Rae was riding in her car seat in the back seat with the windows open on a beautiful warm day with just a small seat belt around her waist. Her mother heard pounding on the roof of the car and Mari-Rae yelling, "Mommy look at me!" Marion looked in the rear view window to see two spindly legs poking through the car window. Mari-Rae sat on the window edge, her entire body except those little legs, sticking out of the car, and pounding on the roof with her fists.

Panicked, Marion, pleaded with her daughter to come back into the car. Traffic whizzed by on either side of the tri-lane highway. No place to pull over. If she stopped too fast, Mari-Rae could tumble out onto the road.

"Please, Mari-Rae." Marion had to stay calm. "Sweetie, come back inside the car."

Mari-Rae pounded harder, giggling with glee, oblivious to the danger.

"Come on now, Mari-Rae," Marion said. "Get back inside." A little louder and desperate, with a rise of panic in her voice.

More pounding on the roof as Mari-Rae kicked the car door with her feet.

Time to change tactics. "Mari-Rae, come in right now! You're going to get hurt."

Marion voice rose to a scream. "NOW, get in this car RIGHT NOW!"

For a second the pounding on the roof stopped. Was she coming in? Marion tried to watch the road, slow the car as much as possible without getting rear-ended and watched the rear view mirror in horror. Still only legs in the view finder.

"MARI-RAE SOPPER. DAMNIT! GET THE FUCK BACK IN THE CAR!" Marion's heart pounded out of her chest.

Only when Mari-Rae was good and ready, did she finally slip back in the window and plop herself down on the seat, grinning from ear to ear from an antic that could have killed her.

The next day Marion had air conditioning installed so she could keep the windows shut.

Little sister, Lynn, was born July 20, 1968. Two-year-old Mari-Rae was very gentle with her baby sister, but she was also jealous. Having just conquered toilet training, she reverted back to soiling her pants. Easier to just put her back in diapers. Sometimes she would tell Grandma Dahlstrom to "put her *(Lynn)* down." When Marion and Bill split up the following September and Marion went to work full time by November, Mari-Rae didn't understand what was happening to her safe little home.

By 1969, Marion was newly divorced, living in a duplex, and raising two girls as a single parent. "Where's Daddy? When is he coming home? I want my Daddy!" Mari-Rae cried herself to sleep. She was too little to grasp the idea of divorce.

Marion recalls sending three-year-old Mari-Rae outside to play in the fenced yard of their duplex on Grissom Lane on a warm summer day while she dressed younger sister, Lynn. What surprise and terror when Marion stepped into the backyard to find Mari-Rae missing.

"Mari-Rae, where are you?"

"Mommy, look at me!" Where? Marion looked up toward the sound. There she was. Mari-Rae had climbed up the metal supports to the patio cover and was now sitting on top of the cover. Was she practicing her mount to the uneven parallel bars?

When not climbing on something, Mari-Rae loved to sit on Marion's lap learning to read one word at a time using the Chicago Tribune "learn to read comic strip." Even then, she was intense and motivated. She'd beg Marion not to stop even after an hour went by. A quick learner, she was easily reading before she entered kindergarten.

The girls spent a lot of time at Grandma and Grandpa Dahlstrom's farmhouse after the divorce. Without traffic lights, speed limits, or police radar, drivers flew down the blacktop road which was a crossway from Burlington to North Avenue (Route 64) in St. Charles.

Grandma was delivering a wedding cake and asked Mari-Rae if she wanted to "go with." Mari-Rae declined and Grandma began to drive down the driveway to the blacktop road. As she was leaving, two-year-old Mari-Rae changed her mind and ran all the way to the road.

Marion spotted Mari-Rae from the window and glanced at infant Lynn asleep in the bassinet. She ran from the house, waving at Mari-Rae to come back.

Mari-Rae waved back, her sandy mane catching in the wind and blowing into her eyes. She brushed it away with a swipe of her arm. *Oh, goody,* Mari-Rae thought. *A game of Catch Me If You Can.*

"Mari-Rae, come closer to the house."

Mari-Rae looked at her and laughed.

Marion raised her hand in a gesture of *stop*. "Mari-Rae, don't." A car whizzed by. Marion took another step toward Mari-Rae.

Mari-Rae matched it with a step closer to the road.

Marion felt her heart pounding in her ears. "Damn it, Mari-Rae, I'm not kidding. Come back here, away from the road." Marion waved her in the direction of safety. A car sped past, spitting up loose asphalt and blowing leaves and twigs around Mari-Rae's ankles.

"Ouch." Mari-Rae looked down at her ankles and wobbled to catch her balance from the gust of wind.

Marion saw her chance. She sprinted like an Olympic runner. She closed the space between them and lunged at her daughter, collapsing on the gravel drive, scraping her arms, but with Mari-Rae wrapped securely in them.

"Mari-Rae, you're going to be the death of me yet," she heaved.

Mari-Rae squirmed out of her arms, pouting. *Well, that spoiled the game fast.*

A few months after Marion and Bill's divorce in January, 1969, Marion took in a roommate to help with expenses in the duplex she had purchased. First it was Carolyn with her two kids. Carolyn babysat while Marion went to work.

Next came Susie Blake in 1970. Not yet four-years-old, Mari-Rae loved to play Memory©, a board game by Hasbro, with Susie. "It was embarrassing," said Susie. "She could beat me every time. Here was this cute little thing. She looked like an angel. But she could beat the pants off of me." Mari-Rae's photographic memory made for tough competition. She was inquisitive, always asking questions.

"She was like an adult in a child's body," said Susie. "I can see her sitting on the couch pretending to read to Lynn. She was bossy, but not cruel. She had no problem saying she was sorry." Mari-Rae was full of energy. Sometimes Susie would pick the girls up from day care if Marion was working late. "Mari-Rae would never stay in her seatbelt. I didn't have car seats for kids in my car."

Within Her Grasp

A favorite time in the household was when Marion made Swedish pancakes, long pancakes rolled up like a crêpe, or huge batches of macaroni and cheese. Mari-Rae, loved the pancakes and mac and cheese.

Birthdays were the best. Grandma made the best cakes in all of Illinois and she had a special one for Mari-Rae's fourth birthday. The table was decorated in a colorful paper tablecloth covered in colorful balloons. After supper and presents came ice cream and cake.

"Take your cones outside," Marion told the little girls.

Mari-Rae took her cone and stomped out to the back patio. Two-year-old Lynn followed close behind. Lynn followed her everywhere. Sometimes it was fun. Sometimes she was just a copy-cat. Would she follow her back into the house? Mari-Rae slid open the sliding glass door to the slab of concrete in the back yard. Sure enough, Lynn was right on her heels. Mari-Rae waited until her sister was outside, then, she jumped back through the door, and—*Wham!* She slammed the door in her face.

Lynn's eyes filled with tears.

Mari-Rae cracked the door open just enough to let her think she was going to let her enter, but not enough for Lynn to fit her body through.

"Mari-Rae, let me in." Lynn wailed.

Mari-Rae stuck a chocolate coated tongue at her little sister.

Lynn tried to squeeze through the opening. She could barely fit her arm. She heaved on the door, but Mari-Rae was older and determined to taunt her.

"Nana, nana, naaa-naa. You can't come in." Mari-Rae sang in triumph through the opening of the door. In an instant, Lynn shoved her chocolate ice-cream cone through the crack and onto Mari-Rae's chest.

Mari-Rae looked down at the large chocolate stain on her shirt. "Ahhhh!" she screamed, throwing herself on the floor, kicking and screaming.

Lynn took advantage of the unguarded door and pushed it open to get in. Marion came running in from the kitchen. Mari-Rae flailed about on the floor. Was she hurt? Was she bleeding? Marion narrowed her eyes at the chocolate stain smeared across Mari-Rae's chest.

"Lynn Sopper. Did you do this? You ruined your sister's shirt. And it's her birthday. Go to your room until supper is ready."

Lynn burst into tears. "But Mommy— Mari-Rae."

Marion pointed toward the stairs. "Enough, to your room . . . Now!"

She turned to her first born. "It's okay, sweetie. We'll get you a clean shirt."

The howling reduced to a whimper. A small smile turned up the corners of her mouth.

The summer of 1970, Frank grew tired of the bad reception from the old attic antenna in Marion's duplex. Although he and Marion had not married yet, he was there enough to be annoyed by the bad reception. God knows it was probably jarred loose from years of hard Illinois winters.

He hauled the ladder to the side of the house so he could install a new roof antenna. The roofline had a fairly level side and a steep incline to a peak. As he hauled the antenna into place, he was startled by a noise behind him. There, high on the peak of the roof, was four-year-old Mari-Rae.

What was she doing up there? She could get killed.

Frank moved slowly, careful he did not make her move away from him too quickly. "Honey, what are you doing up here?"

"I climbed up," Mari-Rae said proudly.

He inched closer to her. *Please don't step back.* Frank made it to her side. "It's time to go down now, okay?"

She shrugged. Okay. No big deal. She grabbed the top of the ladder, swung herself onto it, and gingerly made her way down to the ground.

The Soppers and Kmineks became one big family on May 15, 1971. Mari-Rae was no longer the big sister. She had a new big brother, Frank, two years older and twin siblings a mere five months younger than she.

This new family was not in Mari-Rae's plan. She didn't want this new family, didn't want a new sister and two new brothers. She missed her Daddy and took it out on her new sister, Christina, for crying over missing her Mommy. *Why couldn't things go back to the way they were?* Not once would she ever call her step-father "Dad." He would always be *Frank* to her. They mixed like oil and vinegar. If Frank said something was blue, Mari-Rae said it was black. If Frank wanted to relax and watch TV, Mari-Rae wanted to practice dancing to her cassette player right in front of the TV.

Mari-Rae started kindergarten at a school near their house on Grissom, but soon transferred to Hunting Ridge Grade School in Palatine when the family moved to their new home on Hudson Drive in Winston Knolls in October of 1971. The Cape Cod style house offered a little more room, but it wasn't much bigger than the duplex.

That first Christmas as a large family, Frank and Marion took all of the kids to Disney World for the Grand Opening. The crowds were humongous. By the time they were halfway to the park, they had closed admission because of too many people. They had to turn back and spend the day at the hotel pool. The following day, they left the hotel at four a.m. to get in line for admittance into the park. Two sleepy parents and five excited, but grumpy children waited impatiently in line. They made it in.

At the end of the afternoon, the kids wanted to go through the haunted house. Marion and Frank surveyed the line. It was at least ten people across and they couldn't even see the end of the line.

"That's it," said Frank. "I'm not standing in anymore lines." Frank headed to a shade tree and a bench to wait while Marion took the five kids and got in line.

Lynn fell asleep on Marion's shoulder. By the time they reached the front of the line, Marion was horrified to find out it was a moving sidewalk to board moving tilt-a-wheel cars. The kids thought it was a fun and scary ride. For Marion, trying to board five children under the age of seven on a moving track into two cars that never stopped moving was terrifying.

On the way home, they stopped at a hotel on New Year's Eve. They had two adjoining rooms. One for the kids, one for adults. The kids were treated to Kentucky Fried Chicken and put to bed. Finally Marion and Frank had some alone time. They ordered room service and had Surf and Turf.

In the morning, they had made it about an hour from the hotel when little Lynn discovered that her blankie had been left in the room. There was no consoling the three-year-old, and they were not going back for it. She screamed for hours. Mari-Rae was surprisingly quiet for a change and didn't add to the tension in a car with a screaming toddler.

Grandma and Grandpa Dahlstrom's farm was one of the best places for a child to play. Lots of wide open area to explore. There were cattle, chickens, and miles of corn fields, flower, and vegetable gardens. Beyond them were the woods. Grandpa Dahlstrom warned the kids about getting lost, but that was a temptation too strong to resist.

While Frank's kids went to visit their mother, Lynn, age four, and Mari-Rae, age six, followed Grandpa Dahlstrom and Buddy, his dog, to check on the cornfields on the farm. He let them ride on the big John Deere tractor, but when he stopped to check on some of the stalks, the girls couldn't resist running through the stalks that felt miles taller than their heads. It was a wonderful place to play hide-n-seek, right up until they realized they were hopelessly lost among the cornfields. Mari-Rae, two years older than Lynn, should have been the clear head. Not so. In a total state of panic, she lost it. Wailing and thrashing about only succeeded in getting her boot stuck in the mud. Lynn caught a quick sight of Buddy, but he bounded off through the rows and out of sight.

"Follow the rows," said younger sister Lynn. She had figured out that the stalks ran in the vertical rows, and if they followed them, sooner or later, they would make it out of the cornfield. Reluctantly, Mari-Rae followed Lynn down the rows, sniffling all the way. At last, they were out of the maze. And there was Grandpa, legs dangling over the side of the tractor, hand over his mouth, trying hard to suppress his fit of laughter at their predicament. Buddy bounded toward them in greeting. Grandpa loved the girls and never would have let them stay lost indefinitely, but it was a lesson better learned by experience than by lecture.

Mari-Rae started first grade at Hunting Ridge School in Palatine. The structure must have been good for her. The outbursts experienced at home disappeared in school. "She was an adorable child," said her teacher, Mrs. Barb Tsutsumi. "She was a strong-willed child, which I considered to be a positive quality and one of her strengths." She would study people and listen attentively to lessons. One child was having trouble understanding the lesson plan. Mari-Rae observed for a bit; then she went over and helped explain it. She loved being a part of every activity and watched out for classmates. Her long, sandy hair would get in her eyes and she'd brush it away with a sweep of her arm. "She was inquisitive, funny, affectionate and caring," said Barb.

A school nurse gave Mari-Rae an eye test and called Marion. They scheduled an appointment for an optometrist. On the way home with her first pair of glasses, Mari-Rae pointed. "Look, Mommy. That sign says 35." Marion had no idea that Mari-Rae hadn't been able to see.

The three girls took tap dance and ballet at the Dolores Eihler studio and later at the Bonnie Lindholm studio. The front yards became the playground for all of the neighborhood kids. Mari-Rae, Lynn and Christina became good friends with Dawn Testo (Hichew), who was Mari-Rae and Christina's age and lived across the street. They danced together at the Bonnie Lindholm studio and performed in parades and local civic functions. "The rehearsals leading up to the recitals were the most exciting," said Dawn. They had to practice for two or three days straight, sometimes not getting home until after dark. The girls gossiped together in the back seats while the parents car-pooled. Who liked whom, who was best in the performance, and who was messing up. There was lunch together before rehearsals and fun for all of the girls.

The days of the recital were electric. After each performance, the girls got flowers from their parents and grandparents. Everyone went together to celebrate at Swenson's, the local ice cream parlor.

"Mari-Rae taught me how to do an aerial cartwheel and a back hand spring on her front lawn," said Dawn. It was a good time when children could roam the safe mid-west neighborhood, run in and out of each other's homes, play tag, and run through lawn sprinklers.

In 1974, when Mari-Rae was eight years old, they moved again to the big house on Canterbury Lane in Barrington. For the first time, Mari-Rae had a room of her own when Lynn and Christina agreed to bunk together. It was a great neighborhood with a private community pool for cooling off on hot summer days. The kids fought all the time, and Marion was a yeller herself. The girls cracked their solid six- panel bedroom doors from slamming them so hard. The boys wrestled until the light fixtures shook from the ceiling. Their little cockapoo, Coco, was one pup extraordinaire. His great feat was bounding down the stairs and jumping from the fifth step to hit the handle of the front storm door, escaping from the chaos.

The move meant yet another change in schools to Marion Jordan Elementary School in Palatine.

2   Pre-teen Years - Once Upon a Dream

"I competed because I loved gymnastics. All I wanted to do was gymnastics. I didn't compete because I wanted to make history." Nadia Comãneci[1]

"Mom!" Lynn screamed at the top of her lungs from her spot on the floor in front of the small color television. "The boys are fighting upstairs. The ceiling and the TV are shaking. Tell them to stop." Books teetered precariously on the shelves above the TV. The ceiling light shook and flickered. She sat cross-legged on the beige carpet, slightly stained by five kids snacking on the family room floor. Mari-Rae sat beside her, as transfixed as her sister.

"Frankie, Chris, knock it off." Marion hollered up the stairs. The trembling ceiling stopped for a minute, then resumed. Marion shrugged and headed back into the kitchen. Since marrying Frank Kminek, her family had grown from three to seven. She quickly learned to choose her battles wisely.

The 1976 Olympics were in full swing and Nadia Comãneci had just completed her routine on the uneven parallel bars. Had there ever been anything so beautiful?

---

[1] told to Carmel Dominic of fz.com

Nadia executed a high leap from the spring board into a free straddle which was followed by a hurdle over the low bar to catch the high bar. She went right into a kip and then swung into a back hip circle, followed immediately by a perfect handstand. Neither Mari-Rae nor Lynn understood any of those terms, yet, but they would. Mari-Rae would eventually use Nadia's mount during her high school competitions. They held their breath, waiting for the score. Nellie Kim from Russia was ahead with a 9.9. The score showed on the screen. 1.0. What did that mean? For a moment the crowd was silenced. They didn't understand. Then the announcer explained. The computer system didn't have double digits to make a 10, but Nadia had scored a perfect ten. A TEN! The first *ever* in an Olympic competition, and she had done it on a compulsory routine. The crowd went wild.

"Did you see that?" Lynn squealed. "A ten!" Mari-Rae jumped up and hugged her sister.

Christina looked on from the brown sofa under the bay window. Coco, their white cockapoo, wriggled for attention. "Cool," she said, impressed but not as over-the-top about it as ten-year-old Mari-Rae or eight-year-old Lynn.

"I want to learn to do that," Lynn told her mother. Marion didn't know where to find a gymnastics program but she did her research and chose Palatine Park District. All three girls were taking dance but after the Olympics, Marion enrolled them with the Palatine Park District to take gymnastics also. By their second year of gymnastics due to budget and time restraints, the girls had to make a choice. Mari-Rae and Lynn chose gymnastics, Christina chose dance.

Mari-Rae and Lynn took the sport seriously and went to practice for three or four hours every day after school. With working parents, it was a challenge to get them to all of the practices, so Marion and her friend, Annie Hernandez, traded off car-pooling the girls, Mari-Rae, Lynn, and Annie's daughter, Michele. Typical of all pre-teens, there was sometimes bickering, and sometimes they were so exhausted they fell asleep on the way home. Occasionally, the parents stayed to watch the kids practice. "I never met a girl who loved the sport more than Mari-Rae," said Annie Hernandez. Mari-Rae had so much grace on the floor, incorporating her flair for dance in every move. Even as a young girl, Mari-Rae's determination was evident. She gladly helped any of the other girls. Her love for the sport drove her to want the best for everyone.

Joan and Jean Swanson remember babysitting, sometimes for all five children, and sometimes just for Mari-Rae and Lynn when the other kids were at their mother's house. The private neighborhood pool was a welcome respite from the heat of Illinois summers. The girls routinely practiced their twists and flips off the spring board on the low dive. Even then, Joan and Jean were quite impressed with Mari-Rae and Lynn's talent.

Teenager, Jean, watched the girls one evening while the parents were out. They wanted macaroni and cheese. Simple enough. Jean poured the boiled noodles into the strainer in the sink. She proceeded to pour the cheese and milk over the noodles and right down the drain. Mari-Rae and Lynn looked at Jean like she was crazy. "What? She couldn't even make mac and cheese? What kind of babysitter was she?

Mari-Rae fiddled around in her room, digging in the basket for her leotards, getting side-tracked staring at the picture of Nadia Comãneci on the cover of August 1976 Sports Illustrated.

"Hurry up, Mari-Rae," Marion hollered up the stairs, car keys in hand. "Your sister is ready to go." She looked at her watch. It was five-forty-five p.m. Practice started at six.

They were headed for their gymnastics classes at the Palatine Park District.

Coach Terry made them run laps when they were late and Lynn was tired of Mari-Rae always running behind. They'd have to run laps—again.

Hold on. She was coming. Mari-Rae turned back the even numbered pages in the magazine.

"Leave her," Lynn said from the foyer. "That'll teach her a lesson."

They wouldn't dare. They'd wait for her.

"Christina, go up and get her."

"Ahh," Christina whined. "She's always late. Why should I go get her? She knows you're waiting. I agree with Lynn. Leave her."

"Leave her, leave her." Lynn and Christina chanted at the bottom of the stairs.

"We're leaving." Marion gave one last plea. "I mean it."

The sound of the door slamming perked up Mari-Rae's ears. *Watch, next Mom will blow the horn.*

Yep, just as expected. Mari-Rae could hear the engine running as her mother leaned on the horn. Then the unthinkable happened. They left her. They really left her.

Mari-Rae flew down the stairs and flung open the door. They were gone. Christina looked up from the TV show she was watching.

"Told 'ya," Christina said in a sing-song voice from the family room. "What took you so long?"

Mari-Rae didn't answer. She felt the rage building up in her body. It boiled within her like a volcano. How dare they? How could they really leave her?

She dashed into the family room, exploding with indignation. She couldn't believe it. She screamed at the top of her lungs. She'd show them. With a hurricane of fury, she toppled end tables. *Wham!* With a wide sweep of her arm, the books on the shelf scattered to the floor. *Thud*! Christina's eyes widened in disbelief as Mari-Rae kicked the coffee table over, its legs poking up toward the ceiling, its contents strewn about the room. Coco ran for his life and hid under the couch.

After the fury settled into a calm, Mari-Rae devised a plan. She'd get to practice on her own. She didn't need them. And they'd never know how she did it.

Thirty minutes later, she strode into the gym, a smug look of satisfaction on her face.

Lynn's mouth dropped open in amazement.

"How did you get here? Did your Mom drop you off?" Coach Sandy knew that Marion had just been there dropping Lynn off. Did Mari-Rae call someone to drive her? Did she hitchhike? *Dear God, don't let her have hitchhiked*. She looked out of the window. It was pitch black.

Mari-Rae waved away the question with a shrug.

"Go stretch out, Mari-Rae, and then run laps," Coach Terry said with a frown.

Mari-Rae moved to a corner to flex and warm up. After her laps, she joined the group working on beam. Her movements were graceful. As she vaulted onto the beam and went into an *almost* perfect spin, she saw Sandy nod her approval.

Frank, her step-father picked them up after practice.

"Mari-Rae was late for practice. Mom left without her," Lynn spouted.

"What? Then how did you get there?" Frank frowned at Mari-Rae in the front seat. Mari-Rae's confidence began to waiver. She crouched down lower in the seat and didn't answer. What would happen when they saw what she had done?

Well, they deserved it. They never should have left me.

She tried to scoot up to her room before Frank made it into the family room. Nope. No such luck. It looked like a robbery from a B-rated movie. "Mari-Rae, what have you done?"

"She LEFT me! Why'd she do that? I was ready!" She crossed her arms across her chest and kicked some books across the floor.

"Damn-it, Mari-Rae. That's it. You'd better have this cleaned up before your mother gets home."

Normally she didn't listen to anything Frank had to say. But she knew she had crossed the line. She shoved things back on to the bookshelves in jumbled piles and stacked everything else on the righted coffee table. "There!" She stomped up the stairs.

Well, she showed them. They wouldn't be leaving her again.

Palatine Park Districts Gymnastics was a USGF *(United States Gymnastics Federation)* competitive club. They competed against all of the other USGF private clubs around the Chicago area. While Lynn had more natural ability, Mari-Rae had more dedication. Usually, she scored higher than her little sister from pure determination. During the times he was living in the area, their father, Bill Sopper, was in the stands to cheer them on with whatever wife he had at the time on his arm. He rode the same emotional highs and lows as Mari-Rae, finding life-long companions a struggle. Perhaps that is why the kinship between Mari-Rae and her dad was so tight. The girls spent every weekend with him when not competing.

One time Lynn beat Mari-Rae in a Palatine Park District Club Regional competition. Mari-Rae couldn't be consoled, crying for two days straight. She was a failure, even though she had placed high and both had qualified for State. She didn't begrudge Lynn for being good. It was her own failure—she didn't work hard enough.

Summers for Mari-Rae and Lynn meant Camp Tsukara. It opened in 1974 at Lake Owen in the area of Cable, Wisconsin. Four hundred miles from Chicago, gymnastics camp in the summer, snow-mobile and cross country ski resort in the winter; it was a natural wonderland. Akin to the vacation destination in the movie, *Dirty Dancing,* it was far from roughing it. The big, open lodge had natural hardwood floors and open beams. Dorms, or cabins, housed bunks for the kids, and a huge boys' dorm housed seventy boys at a time.

Some people would argue that Title IX had nothing to do with the burst of interest in women's gymnastics. Title IX is a portion of the United States Education Amendments of 1972 that stated (in part): *No person in the United States shall, on the basis of gender, be excluded from participation in, be denied the benefits of, or be subjected to discrimination under any education program or activity receiving federal financial assistance.*

Regardless of varied opinions of the political implication, women's gymnastics took a huge leap in recognition. After the 1972 Olympics with Olga Korbut, the Soviet gymnast who took three golds in spite of a terrible fall, and in 1976, with Romanian, Nadia Comãneci scoring that first perfect 10.0, gymnastics soared to its peak in popularity. Camp Tsukara was one of the first camps of its kind. Big name gymnasts like Kurt Thomas and other Olympians signed on as counselors. Parents and kids scrambled to get in line for camp.

Lynn and Mari-Rae both trained at Camp Tsukara when Mari-Rae was twelve (1978) and Lynn was ten. They rode a bus from Maine East High School in Park Ridge, Illinois, in the Chicago area where the camp picked up all of the kids from the surrounding areas. It was a long trip, taking over eight hours. The early hours were full of excitement and chatter, but near the end, the bus was relatively quiet.

The girls stayed for three weeks their first year, and then called home, begging to stay all summer, which they did. They returned for every summer thereafter. Cabins were named for Olympic cities, and the first year, they both were housed in cabin Tokyo. Shaun Hoffmeyer was their cabin counselor that first year. Others like Julie and Joann Morris from New Orleans and Deb Bryant

Janssen from Iowa would spend every summer with them.

Eighty miles of national forest encircled the camp. Cold, crystal clear lakes were sometimes still frozen over when camp started in June. The air was fresh and smelled of pine. The program was structured, with three hours of gymnastics in the morning, lunch and an hour rest in their cabins, then back to their routines or classes from one to four-thirty and Open Gym from four-thirty to six every day. Evenings, after a healthy meal, the kids participated in talent shows and skits, Frisbee tosses, or a lively game of volleyball. During each session, they had a contest. On a particular Friday, there was a handstand contest. The person who could hold the handstand the longest won. With experienced gymnasts, this could last a long time. One by one, they fell by the wayside. At last there was only one—Mari-Rae. The prize? Smashing a pie into the face of any counselor of her choice. Mari-Rae chose Mike Jacki, owner/operator of the camp. Mike stood on a stool. First she taunted him with it, waving it around in front of him. He'd wince, squinting shut his eyes and setting his jaw. Not yet. She waited for him to open his eyes. He relaxed his stance. He opened his mouth when—*Bam!* She smashed the whipped cream pie in his face. The whole camp was in stitches.

Saturday night meant camp dances for the teens. Sundays were the only day off, with morning church for those inclined to attend and getting dressed up for meals.

Structure was the key to success with a hundred kids at a time on the premises. Many Iowa State students served as counselors. Rules were strictly enforced. No boys upstairs in the girls' dorms. No one in their cabins or dorms during the day, except for room-cleaning and rest hour. Most equipment was outside; men's rings suspended from trees, spring boards and trampolines in the fresh northern air. A seven thousand-square-foot pole barn housed some of the girls' equipment: the uneven bars and a spring board floor system for floor exercises.

Mari-Rae was in her element, enjoying the rigorous routine, never afraid to ask for help. She showed up to camp with a list of things to accomplish, quite a feat for a child of twelve or thirteen. "I need you to help me," she cried to Mike Jacki. "Here are the four tricks I need to learn." While most kids arrived thinking this was a fun way to spend the summer, she tackled it like a job.

Normally late for everything, when morning practice started at nine a.m., Mari-Rae was there at eight-forty-five. After lunch and rest, stretching started at one-forty-five. Mari-Rae was there at one-thirty. She was a girl on a mission.

3 Fremd High School - A Rising Star

"It all started with her. Mari-Rae put Fremd on the map." Coach Larry Petrillo

Larry Petrillo first met Mari-Rae at a meet at Fremd High School when he was assistant coach at Arlington Heights, a rival high school in the area. Her reputation had already preceded her as a force with which to be reckoned. Fremd High School Gymnastics needed some help. Mari-Rae could be that missing element. During Mari-Rae's freshman year, the team was 0-13. The stands were pretty empty.

Spring break during freshman year, Marion took the three girls, Lynn, Christina, and Mari-Rae, and headed south for some sun. Frank stayed back with the boys, and later started their own tradition with "man time." Money was tight and the girls only had a thousand dollars for the entire week. Between the girls in the back seat was a cooler with soda pop and food. They brought with them an electric frying pan to cook whatever wasn't sandwiches and snacks. They stopped at a motel with a pool and stayed for a few days enjoying the sun and the pool. At night, they cooked popcorn in the frying pan. Someone there told them about Gulf Shores, Alabama. It sounded good, so they headed for Gulf Shores.

When they arrived, the town didn't look anything like they expected. A hurricane had come through a year or two before, and much of the town was a ghost town with blue tarps covering rooftops and many closed establishments. Well, they'd come this far. Might as well make the best of it. They finally found a hotel that was still open for business. It had one room left, with two small beds.

"It's okay," said Mari-Rae. "I'll sleep on the floor." Right. That didn't happen, but they did take the room. They had a great time and the beach was fantastic. The warm weather held out and without any major meltdowns by any of the teenagers, it was a good vacation.

When Coach Petrillo was approached by Fremd principal, Tom Howard, about being the head coach at Fremd the following year, he was delighted. It wasn't until later that Coach Petrillo learned it was Mari-Rae who had approached Principal Howard and told him he "had to hire Coach Petrillo." It appears that even school principals listened to little five-foot-two Mari-Rae.

When Coach Petrillo, sometimes called "Coach P," or even just "P," came on board her sophomore year as the new head coach for men's and women's gymnastics, Mari-Rae already had a plan. Of course he had his own plans, routines, and skills to teach the girls.

Mari-Rae was not the best gymnast on the team, but she tried the hardest. Near the end of her freshman season, she landed wrong while trying to learn a Tsukahara vault. Mari-Rae and the coach both heard a crack. Not good. She had hurt her ankle very badly. She hoped for a bad sprain. She came home and iced and elevated it. The next day, when she got out of bed, she let out a blood-curdling scream. She couldn't put any weight on that ankle. Frank, her step-father, took off of work and took her to their sports doctor, while her mother was out showing homes.

"It's broken," the doctor explained.

"No! It can't be. I have to compete!" Mari-Rae cried.

"Look, Mari-Rae," he said. "Your health has to come before the meets. But if you can put your weight on it, I'll wrap it instead of cast it."

"I can, I swear I can." She stood and tried to place her full weight on it. Down she went. The pain ripped all the way into her gut. Tears coursed down her cheeks.

The cast went on. She missed the end of the season.

Mari-Rae's sophomore year, she approached the coach. "P," she said. "I think we can win District this year, and place at State by next year, and *win* State in my senior year."

Wow, talk about optimistic. Every week, she brought Coach a detailed list of who needed to improve in what area. She knew all of her teammates' strengths and weaknesses. If Ashley would only spring a little higher when she did her back flip on the beam. Tisha had a powerful vault but she needed help on floor. She didn't have the majestic flair that Mari-Rae had. Denise had a bit of a temper and rarely listened to anything anyone would say. She laughed in Mari-Rae's face, which only infuriated her and made her stomp off in frustration.

Frictions ran high on the team, but Mari-Rae didn't give up. She meant well. She only wanted everyone to be the best that they could be. Her motives were never selfish or intended to hurt anyone's feelings.

They had a common goal. Even as they rolled their eyes and walked away, eventually they listened and improved.

Mari-Rae was mostly patient, anxious to see the girls succeed, but her suggestions were not always met with enthusiasm. Her zeal often meant she would get up in the girls' faces. "Come on, you can do better than that. Try harder. Why don't you try a twist? You need to flow with the music."

Why couldn't they understand she was only trying to help? She could make them better, the team better. They could be a winning team. Bewildered, Mari-Rae was met with less-than-enthusiastic appreciation for her pointers. Inside, she was crushed, but she put on a good face for them. *Never let them see her cry.* And Coach didn't stand for theatrics in the gym. But frustration turned to self-loathing. What was wrong? Why couldn't she get through to them? Was she being unreasonable?

Mari-Rae was a natural at dance during her floor and beam routines. Gymnasts stopped and took notice when she was on the floor. It was a sight of beauty and grace. It wasn't long before she was choreographing many of the girls' floor and beam routines.

Weekends were getting harder and harder to visit her Dad. He was still in the stands for some of her meets, by now with his fifth wife, Kathy. Just knowing he was there made her feel loved.

Never could there be a more unlikely friendship than Mari-Rae and Denise. They were exact opposites. Mari-Rae showed a side to Denise that many of the other girls never saw. Denise recalled first meeting Mari-Rae years before at an open gym at the local YMCA. They reconnected on the Fremd gymnastics team. Denise didn't run in the same crowd with Mari-Rae. While

Mari-Rae was a "club kid," training at the Palatine Park District gym, Denise practiced at the YMCA. Mari-Rae was intense and focused, Denise was carefree and distracted. Mari-Rae had a tall sense of right and wrong, and expected everyone to live up to her ideals. She'd find Denise in the "smoker's corner" of the school.

"You have to stop that." Mari-Rae would shake a finger at her.

Denise only laughed. While the other girls got angry with Mari-Rae's attempt to show them how they could improve, Denise shrugged it off.

"You're not taking this serious enough," said Mari-Rae.

"So?" Denise said. She knew that gymnastics was not the end-all for her. There was life outside of gymnastics.

Denise and Mari-Rae frequently could be found huddled together at the top of the stairwell to the "shelf," the upper deck of the gymnasium that housed the gymnastic equipment. The other girls stepped over them, giggling and laughing as they ran down the stairs. The audacity of Mari-Rae. Who did she think she was?

Despite her poised and determined exterior, life was not always easy for Mari-Rae. Her resolve evaporated. "Why?" Mari-Rae asked Denise again and again. There, in the stairwell, or in the empty locker room, Mari-Rae let her down her guard to her friend Denise, who wrapped an arm around her shoulder. And the tears flowed. Nobody understood her. She was hardest on herself. If the team was not at its best, Mari-Rae took it as a personal failure. Every disappointment was met with insecurity and depression. As high as her peaks were when things went according to plan, the lows eclipsed them.

That same year was her first love. What teenage girl story would be complete without a boy? But when Mari-Rae was struck with the love bug, she approached it with the same gusto as competition. He was now part of the plan. He was her dream come true. She followed him to class.

Little response.

She found every party where he would be and made sure she was there.

A polite brush-off.

She called him—a lot. Finally, he asked her out. They dated for a while, but then Mari-Rae started telling him "the plan." She knew where they'd go to college together, when they'd get married, how many kids they'd have.

Whoa! Back up. He wasn't ready for that.

They dated through the end of the year. They discussed prom and decided that neither one wanted to go. They could always go the next year.

For spring break that year, the "girls," Marion, Mari-Rae, Lynn, and Christina went back to Gulf Shores. The town had improved since the year before, restaurants and motels were in better shape, and the town was thriving again. That year they secured two rooms. One restaurant that they frequented was named the same as *him*. Mari-Rae liked going there because it was the name of her first love.

The team ended the season with a record of 4–6, rising from 0–13 the year before. It was a major accomplishment which evoked pride in everyone. In spite of her volatile moods, Mari-Rae knew how to make them win. What she lacked in stature, she made up for in intensity. She even chose which leotards and warm-ups they'd have for the following year .Mari-Rae made the decisions. Not even Coach Petrillo questioned her now. Her plan was falling in place.

At District, Mari-Rae placed second in All-Around and first on uneven parallel bars and floor. She made the cut on bars and qualified to compete in the State Finals. Her routine had a high degree of difficulty with a challenging mount onto the uneven parallel bars. With a high leap from the spring board into a free straddle, she'd hurdle over the low bar and catch the high bar, going into a kip. She'd never had trouble with it before. But during the State finals, she missed, grabbing the low bar and hung there. For a moment, time stood still. She looked over at her coach.

"P, what do I do?" A mortified look crossed her face as if she was naked in front of the world. Of course there was nothing to do but get up and continue the routine. But the low score knocked her into tenth place of the competition.

School was coming to a close. And so was the first love of her life. He did the unforgiveable. He broke it off. She begged. She pleaded. When that didn't work, she crumbled. Denise met her in the stairwell where she cried for two hours straight. Why did these things happen to her? What did she do wrong?

Mari-Rae didn't know how to let it go. She followed him like she did in the beginning. Denise told her that she had to stop—it was stalking, pure and simple.

"But I love him," Mari-Rae cried to her.

By the end of her sophomore year, as each kid was given his or her yearbook, Mari-Rae and Denise sat huddled in the stairwell again, reminiscing over the school year. Mari-Rae took a marker and circled *his* photo in Denise's yearbook—every single photo: class picture, sports photo, candid shots. Every time *he* was photographed, Mari-Rae circled it in the book. Some say you never get over that first love.

Mari-Rae held out hopes that he would show up for her sixteenth birthday party that June. A few of her girlfriends and the family were there, but he didn't show. It was over. He started dating another gymnast on the team.

Her younger sister, Lynn, joined the team as a freshman when Mari-Rae was a junior. Lynn had a natural talent that Mari-Rae didn't have. But she was quieter about it and the squeaky wheel syndrome worked well. Mari-Rae was the one who got people's attention. The one thing Mari-Rae did have was determination.

Following the tradition of spring break vacations, in March 1983, the girls—Mom, Lynn, Christina and Mari-Rae and one of their friends—went to a golf and tennis resort south of Orlando. It was supposed to be special girl time for some bonding. One night after a sun-filled day, they drove to a nearby shopping center.

After shopping with four teenage girls, the conversation turned to the prom. Mari-Rae talked her mom into buying her a dress even though she still didn't have a date for the prom. It was perfect. *He,* her first love from sophomore year, would come back and take her to prom. *He* would love it. She just knew it.

Mari-Rae turned to her sisters. "You can't tell anyone at school I bought this dress," she said. "Especially you, Lynn." She pointed her finger at her sister. "Don't you tell anyone!"

Words were exchanged. Mari-Rae slapped Lynn across the face, irate at some off-handed crack she made.

"Stop!" Lynn shouted back at her.

They made it to the car, Mari-Rae and Marion were in the front seat and the other girls were in the back.

Mari-Rae would not let it go. She spun in her seat, facing the back and waving a finger in her sister's face. "I'm telling you, Lynn, you'd better not say anything to *anyone* that I bought this dress. You'll ruin everything."

"Get your finger out of my face," Lynn shouted back at her. "STOP POINTING YOUR FINGER AT ME! Mom, I'm warning her."

Marion groaned. "Girls, stop."

Mari-Rae reached across the back of the seat and slapped Lynn again in the face.

Lynn reacted before she even had time to think. *Pow!* She punched Mari-Rae right in the face. *Pow!* Before Mari-Rae could even react, she punched her again.

Aaaaa! Mari-Rae burst into tears and jumped from the moving car, right in the middle of parking lot. She took off running across the dark lot, screaming and crying hysterically. All the stores had closed by then and no one was around to see or surely someone would have suspected child abuse.

After following her for a bit, Marion turned off the engine and they waited. She'd have to come back soon. It was dark. It was deserted. They were in a strange town. There was nowhere to go.

Finally Mari-Rae slipped back into the front seat. She needed ice. They drove to a near-by movie theatre and Marion got a cup of ice for her face. The following day they drove home from Florida. She showed up at school the following Monday with a black eye.

As for the saga of the prom? She was invited to prom by a boy with whom she was friends but never actually dated. But prior to the dance, she started seeing someone else. It didn't go over well with either of the boys. Her prom date backed out and her new boyfriend broke up with her. She never wore the dress.

Fremd High School had a winning team by the time Mari-Rae was a senior. The stands were full for meets. Each year, new captains of the team were voted in by ballot among the girls. Mari-Rae was sure she was a shoe in. She had brought them this far.

When the ballots were totaled, Susie, a junior, was voted Captain.

What? No, that couldn't be right. Mari-Rae dashed from the room in tears. "I can't believe this. How can this be? Why do you hate me?"

Coach Petrillo was baffled. He didn't expect this. Was it spite? Susie was an outstanding gymnast, but look how Mari-Rae had brought the team to where they were. He sat the girls down and talked to the team, feeling like he had misdirected them as their coach.

"Girls, we all know how Mari-Rae can be. But you also know what she has done for this team. I should have told you to vote for a senior for your Captain. It's only right." Begrudgingly, the girls all agreed. Mari-Rae and Susie would be Co-Captains. They would give her that.

The next day, Mari-Rae showed up for practice, swallowing her pride and taking it for the team. Coach Petrillo first explained to Susie that she had another year to be Captain. Then he pulled Mari-Rae aside and explained it was his error, that only seniors should have been eligible to be Captain. Since Susie had already been elected, they would share the title and responsibilities. Mari-Rae was not convinced, but she nodded, squared her shoulders and headed to the mat. Susie, being an intelligent young girl, understood the situation. She'd let Mari-Rae run the program, settling for the title in name only.

Mari-Rae was not without further injuries. Her senior year, she hurt her back. Marion took her to a chiropractor who said he would have to see her on a regular basis so she could keep competing. He said it wouldn't do any further damage to compete but it would not heal until she stopped competing. She finished the season in spite of the pain and would continue with her life dream.

After meets, the parents hosted parties in their homes. The adults skirted the kitchen islands laden with food and drink. The kids congregated in the basements with pizza and pop. It wasn't just a gymnastics team. It was a community. As Coach P said, "Winners breed winners." Everyone wanted onboard this train. They were headed toward Mari-Rae's goal of State Champions. Three thousand people filled the stands for the State Meet. The room vibrated with electricity. The girls filed in with exact precision, perfectly in step, heads high, dressed in green and gold, proud to be Fremd Vikings.

It was the State Championship, Mari-Rae's senior year. She and Coach Petrillo had taken the team from an unranked team to the finals. Mari-Rae usually placed first, second or third in the meets. Fremd High School consistently ranked in the top three schools in their district and once again placed second at the State Meet.

Only Mari-Rae was not satisfied. That was not her plan. They should have made first, and she was hardest of all on herself.

Fremd High School voted Mari-Rae MVP, Most Valuable Player. The State presented her with the distinguished trophy for Illinois Outstanding Senior Gymnast. It was an honor only one person in the entire state would receive. At the Senior Award Banquet, Coach Petrillo choked up. "This never would have happened without Mari-Rae. She put Fremd on the map." He and the school would always be grateful for the contribution Mari-Rae made to Fremd and to gymnastics. Her future was looking bright.

What did she leave with Fremd when she headed to Iowa State University? She left the team with the determination and belief in itself to excel and, with her sister, Lynn's help, the team won first in State that next year and for several years thereafter. Mari-Rae was set on her path. She would major in exercise science. She would see her dream come true.

Mari-Rae took a recruiting trip to Ames, Iowa, to visit Iowa State. She was already pretty sure this was the college she wanted to attend. Many of her friends from Camp Tsukara were already there. Junior gymnast, Kathy Edwards (Federico), showed her around the campus. They toured the campus and went to a party, but Mari-Rae was serious, drilling Kathy about the team. "She looked so young," said Kathy. I felt like I needed to take her under my wing.

Mari-Rae had her plan. She would go to Iowa State. She'd major in Exercise Science and someday be a collegiate coach.

4 Iowa State University – Driven by Excellence

"Mari-Rae was the Yin and Yang,"
Kathy Edwards Federico.

Mari-Rae walked onto Iowa State University Gymnastics team with the same enthusiasm she had at Fremd. It was almost like old-home week with so many of her Camp Tsukara friends there, like Mark Diab and Shane Sanders. She moved into the dorm and made her first call.

"Mark, what's up?" she asked enthusiastically.

"Well, I'm having a party," said Mark, "but there won't be any freshman there." He tried to warn her that things may be a little rowdier than when they had last seen each other at Camp Tsukara.

"Not a problem," she said. "I'll bring some of my friends."

Mark groaned under his breath. Now he'd have to look after her like his little sister. This wasn't such a great idea.

When Mari-Rae arrived at the party with her friends, Mark took her aside. "See those guys over by the garage? Steer clear of them. And those guys out back— best to leave them alone, too."

Mari-Rae nodded, listening intently to everything he had to say, her big blue eyes glued in attention to what he said. Then she turned her back and headed straight for the guys by the garage.

"But Mar…." Too late. She was off and running. As the evening wore on, Mark tried to keep tabs on her, but the crowd made it impossible to know where she was at all times.

"Hey, Mark," one of his senior buddies slapped him on the shoulder. "Who's that little thing over there?" He pointed to Mari-Rae, her head barely visible between the shoulders of two big strapping guys. She was adorable, pretty, and petite, comfortable being the center of attention.

"Why?" Something told Mark this wasn't going to be good.

"First, she told one dude he needed to stop smoking. And by the time she was done talking to him, he agreed to give them up. Then, she told this other guy he should get back with his girlfriend and she convinced him to leave the party right now and call her. She should go into politics. She can talk you into anything.

In 1984, college gymnastics was a head count sport. There was a limited amount of money available for scholarships. Iowa State head coach, Donna Kramer, had the philosophy that freshmen should walk-on and earn their chance for a scholarship as upper classmen. Coach Kramer was retiring and Assistant Coach Mike Sharples would take over as head coach the next year.

Coach Mike couldn't have been more pleased to have Mari-Rae as a walk-on. She was a big-name gymnast, her reputation and high school accomplishments already well known. Mike liked to think that he recruited her, but anyone who knew Mari-Rae would wonder about who recruited whom. She had a slender grace and beauty in events. By the end of her freshman year at Iowa State, Mari-Rae's steadfast fortitude had earned an almost full athletic scholarship for her remaining three years at school.

When they started training in August, the wind was blowing and the pollen was at its height. The PE Building didn't have air conditioning and it was about a ten-minute walk from the dorm, hot—about one hundred degrees. Due to her hay fever, Mari-Rae couldn't wear her contacts, so she wore her glasses, which fogged up, and she could hardly see. She bounded into the gym with her nose running, her eyes red and swollen, and talking a mile a minute. "If the gym was open, Mari-Rae was in there," said Coach Mike. She would spend two-and-a-half to three-and-a-half hours a day, five days a week; six during competition.

Mari-Rae expected to walk on the team with the same leadership she had experienced at Fremd High School, but she was in the big leagues now. She was a little minnow in a big pond. She had plans, like always, but they weren't met with the same acceptance to which she had become accustomed by her senior year in high school.

Coach Mike had a different style of coaching than Coach P, coaching individually, not as a group. Mari-Rae didn't always agree. She was smart. She knew the rules and how to put difficult combinations of skills together to improve the scoring for the whole team. She had a photographic memory and could list the scores of all the competitors from every school in the conference. Why couldn't they do things her way?

"It's not fair," she whined to Kathy, her friend who had shown her around on her recruiting trip. She saw the strengths and weaknesses of the team, including herself. She wanted everyone to live by her personal rules of conduct, on and off the gym floor. Her high personal moral code, naïve, was not always conducive to college life. Everyone's dream was not the same as Mari-Rae's. She just couldn't accept that fact.

The pre-season competition, called The Rocky Mountain Open, was held in Colorado Springs at the Air Force Academy. The team flew in two eight-passenger Beech planes owned by Iowa State. Because they had to bring their own spring board, there was barely room for their small duffel bags. They would arrive a day early and spend the night in a hotel. This was done to in order to acclimate to the high altitude which was very difficult, if not impossible, for the Iowa State kids, especially during the floor routines which lasted up to ninety seconds. They'd end up gasping for air, trying to finish their routines. Mari-Rae's strength was her dance in her floor routine, and she could find the most difficult dance skill to score higher. She competed against herself. She could do single back flip with two twists, referred to as a "double full," and do a "double turn," which is performed on one foot with two revolutions completed before putting the second foot on the floor[2], both D-skill level, which was the highest you could do. Mari-Rae and Kathy eyed the beautiful marble trophies, presented by the Air Force Academy.

"I want one of those bird trophies," Kathy said to Mari-Rae.

---

[2] as described by Mike Sharples, Iowa State Coach

"Me, too," said Mari-Rae.

"Ma'am," a handsome Air Force Cadet said, "That would be a falcon."

The girls slinked away, laughing at their gaffe. Happily, they each placed in the meet and received one to take home.

1984 was also the year Mari-Rae turned eighteen. She was eligible to vote. Mari-Rae loved politics and was determined to be the one voice that made a difference. A staunch democrat, she rallied for Walter Mondale and Geraldine Ferraro to win the election. It was of little use as Ronald Reagan and George H. Bush won by a landslide in the November elections.

Mari-Rae was assigned to mentor a new recruit on a visitation trip. She took high school student Julie Sullivan (Soldat) under her wing, just as Kathy had done for her. She gave her the tour of the school, and later took her to a party. "She let me have fun," Julie said. "She *(Mari-Rae)* was mellower than me," said Julie. "But she didn't cramp my style. She just watched over me and made sure she had my back."

Mari-Rae did her personal best with a 9.25 on March 2, 1985, her freshman year, on floor exercise against Southern Illinois. Her grace as a dancer shined on floor and beam. She let no one settle for mediocre. It wasn't in her vocabulary. She was never afraid to aim high. Her enthusiasm was infectious and the team soared with her leadership. She raised the bar of excellence for the whole team. Even her senior teammates, like Deb Diskerud (Hatanpa) soon looked toward Mari-Rae for her inspiration. Mari-Rae should have been looking toward upper classmen like Deb to set the example, but it was the other way around.

"Mari-Rae's dedication and encouragement were part of the reason I started putting harder tricks into my routines during my last competitive season," said Deb. "Finally, as a senior, I started taking a few risks after several years of 'coasting' through routines that I could do in my sleep."[3]

Seniors, Debbie Diskerud, Mimi Starts, and Sara Krause brought their leadership to the team that year. Kathy Edwards (Federico), a junior, made MVP, setting records in vault, bars, floor, and all-around.

When Julie enrolled the fall of 1985, she and Mari-Rae formed a friendship that would last a lifetime. They lived in the same dorm and spent as much time together outside of the gym as in the gym. Mari-Rae roomed with a fellow teammate her sophomore year, but outside of the gym, they had little in common, so Mari-Rae frequently found herself in Julie's room hanging out.

Sunday was their special day together. Once a week, Sundays only, Mari-Rae would treat herself to something different from her usual health-food regime of a salad. Julie and Mari-Rae went to the local Dairy Queen where Mari-Rae would order a huge Blizzard for dinner, or they'd walk to Doughbiz, the local bakery. Mari-Rae's favorite decadent delight was a huge chocolate chip cookie, eight inches around and a half-inch thick.

Mari-Rae laughed at her friend, Julie, when she showed up in a pea coat identical to her own. In truth, Julie idolized Mari-Rae. She nicknamed Mari-Rae "LaMar," from La M-R. Julie cut her hair to look like

---

[3] Mari-Rae Sopper Memorial Website

LaMar. She bought the same clothes and mimicked her actions.

Mari-Rae's friends dubbed her car "the LaMar mobile." Once when she was driving home with several college friends, they all fell asleep, including Mari-Rae, who was driving. They woke up to hear *thud, thud, thud*, which was the sound of cornstalks hitting the car as they drove through a cornfield. Thank God for the Midwest where there was little obstruction for miles on end.

Mari-Rae was the marquee player on the team. Even if she wasn't the most talented and didn't place the highest, she became the poster girl for the girls' gymnastics team and they used her photo shots for promotional materials. They gave her the coveted cover photo for the Iowa State Gymnastics magazine two years in a row.

The team worked on skills in groups, with assistant coaches keeping everyone moving. They worked on tumbling in the tumbling pit. The girls raced down the padded and carpeted runway strip into a giant pit of foam boxes which let them work on their tumbling skills without injury. A spring floor was state-of-the-art for floor routines, and padded beams replaced the hard wood ones used in high school.

Mastering a "Tsuk" *(tsukahara)* vault was not one of her strongest skills. Multiple times she tried and failed to perform the vault to her satisfaction. She planted her feet on the lines, making sure her toes were exactly on the edge of the line. Then she stretched out her arm and aligned herself with the wall. She adjusted her leotard twice. She tapped her legs twice. She ran her middle fingers across her eyebrows. And off she went, arms swinging. She sprinted down the runway and jumped on the spring board, did her half-turn onto the horse, and then was supposed to push off completing a flip (a.k.a., a backward salto) landing on her feet. She almost always landed on her knees.

She'd start again. Line up her toes. Align with the wall. Adjust her leotard twice. Tap her legs twice. Then she was off. And she landed on her knees again. Her practices had to fit into her "even numbers" superstition. Even if Coach Mike wanted three bars and five vaults, she always did even sets. Not an option to do otherwise.

She showed up to practice early and was always last to leave, quite a change from her youth when she was always late. Her quest for perfection exceeded her natural talent, but she didn't take failure lying down. Julie and Kathy tried to make her laugh at herself. LaMar was doing fine. Soon the whole team was calling her LaMar.

Mari-Rae laughed it off, but that didn't stop her focus. She was going to learn that vault. Coach tried to lighten the mood and make her more relaxed. He imitated her moves, swiping his brow, pretending to adjust a leotard and tap his legs. She stomped around, huffing and puffing, trying to be mad. Then she'd settle down, adjust her leotard twice, tap her legs twice, and swipe her brows with her middle fingers before trying again.

"Maybe you should try a vault with a lower degree of difficulty," Coach Mike suggested.

"We need the higher degree to keep our points up."

Not if you can't make it. Mike thought to himself, but never would have said that out loud.

Then one day Mari-Rae had the answer. She had poured over the rule book and found a different vault with the same level of difficulty that she could master.

She could do a half-twist off the springboard onto the vault and then a full-twist after the dismount instead of a tucked backwards salto. And just like that, she mastered it.

She'd walk in to every practice ready to go. She expected everyone to commit to the same dedication as she did. She believed in them and wanted to see them succeed. She would never undercut her teammates. She had no malice, even when it was not always taken that way. She also did her best all-around score of 35.70 on March 27, 1986, against Nebraska her sophomore year.

In November of 1985, Iowa State's men's and women's cross-country teams had NCAA National Championships in Milwaukee, Wisconsin. It was a great meet and the women took second place nationally. The teams were jubilant and anxious to get home to their families for Thanksgiving, just three days away. Three of the university's small planes carried the teams and their coaches. The weather was bad. Air traffic controllers re-routed the planes through Des Moines. One plane, carrying the coach, assistant coach, three of the women's team members and a trainer experienced difficulty with ice forming on the wings. The pilot issued a May-Day alert just minutes before the plane crashed into a residential neighborhood in Des Moines. All on board were killed. Fortunately, no one on the ground was hurt. The other two planes landed safely at the Des Moines airport. The entire school was in a state of shock. It was not the kind of excitement anyone wanted before heading home for the holidays. The gymnastics teams never flew in the small planes again. They took commercial airlines.[4]

---

[4] E-library@Iowa State University, Stu Beiter, Gendisators.com, Dec. 23, 2002, Oelwein Daily Register, Nov. 26, 1985

That same year, they closed the dorms during Christmas and Spring Breaks. The team had to stay on campus to practice so the school put them up in the Gateway Hotel for three weeks at Christmas and one week during Spring Break. Coach Mike had rules. No boys in the girls' hotel rooms. During one such hotel stay, the girls were making signs for the next meet. Some of the boys showed up to help and Mari-Rae reported them. They had broken the rules. In her mind, it was simple, black and white. Mari-Rae had no gray areas.

Coach Mike had no choice but to enforce punishment for the crime. The boys and girls involved were not allowed to compete in the meet in Oklahoma. With only four or five team members left, they didn't stand a chance. The meet was a disaster. Some of the boys' and girls' team members were not about to forget who cost them the meet. True, they had made the infraction, but if Mari-Rae hadn't blown the whistle on some innocent sign-making, they might have won. Some eventually forgave her, others did not.

She also reported one of her team members who was on a full scholarship for using drugs. The girl lost her scholarship and because her family didn't have the money to pay for out-of-state tuition and room and board, she had to leave school.

"Mari-Rae was the Yin and Yang," said Kathy.

Even numbers weren't Mari-Rae's only idiosyncrasies. One of her other "rules" was no hair products on Sunday. She said it was her hair's day of rest. And no studying on the bed; only at the desk. Mari-Rae's quirks endeared her to her friends and sometimes put off others. "It was what made Mari-Rae, Mari-Rae. We loved her," said Julie.

Mari-Rae was a beautiful girl and men were of no shortage. Getting a boyfriend was the easy part. Keeping one was another story. She thought she finally had "Mr. Right" after dating a guy on campus for six months. He was everything she wanted—handsome, out-going, funny, Mr. Joe-Cool around campus. Then suddenly it was over. No explanation. No long goodbye. It was just over. Mari-Rae was devastated—again.

"Why?" She cried to Julie and Kathy. "What did I do wrong? We had everything going for us." This wasn't part of her plan. No one had an answer for her. All they could do was wrap her in love and let her cry. Would this be a recurring theme? Was she like her father, unable to hold on to a relationship?

Good friend and fellow gymnast, Shane Sanders, was usually nearby to pick up the pieces whenever things didn't go as planned. One such time he tried to cheer her up with some soft serve ice cream at the Quik-Trip. The directions were a picture on the machine. It was simple. Put the cone under the faucet and pull the handle. The picture showed a perfect cone with swirling soft serve curly tip.

"I can't do that!" Mari-Rae cried.

Shane looked at her, puzzled. "What are you talking about? You just put the cone under the nozzle and pull."

"I can't," she whined. "Do it for me, please?" She batted her big eyes at him.

"No, don't be ridiculous. There's nothing to it. Do it yourself." Shane looked away.

When he turned back toward her, she had ice cream running up both arms, and blobs of ice cream all over the floor and not a drop in her cone.

"See, see. I told you I can't do it."

Mari-Rae could talk people into (or out of) just about anything. When she decided to prove a point, she did it with gusto.

Scoring for college gymnastics had only two decimals. She was one of the first to start scoring 9's consistently, but she never made the elusive 10.0.

The NCAA Big 8 Conference had only a few schools with gymnastic teams. Iowa State competed with Nebraska, Oklahoma, Missouri, and Oklahoma State. Because there wasn't a full complement of schools in their conference, they also went to out-of-conference meets like University of Iowa, SEMO *(South East Missouri)*, Southern and Northern Illinois, and Minnesota

For home games, they moved bleachers into 194 PEB (Physical Education Building[5]), a new building on campus, before meets until they filled it up. By the time Mari-Rae was a senior, they had to move the meets into the main arena at Hilton Coliseum on campus. Energy was high. Two events went on at a time, both teams performing at the same time on different events.

On vaults, each girl did two vaults. The judges scored both vaults and the teams used the higher of the two scores as the score for that gymnast. On floor routine, they had one shot, as well as bars and beam. Mari-Rae was an all-arounder and did all four events. Some girls only competed in one or two events. The top

---

[5] since renamed to the Barbara Folker Building

five out of six gymnasts' scores were then totaled for each event to calculate the team's score.

Although they rarely won, the scores were always high and they were in a strong conference, so it helped to raise their national rankings. Mari-Rae was frustrated that they were not winning, even though she was placing first, second, or third, but she was pleased as long as they competed with tough schools and their rankings continued to rise. Coach Mike's philosophy was that in order to be one of the top teams in the country, they needed to compete against the powerhouse teams, like the SEC teams and Utah, rather than a schedule in which they were bound to win. Teams' average scores were the determining factor in Regional Championships, not win-loss records. Mari-Rae shared his belief that the team should compete with the best. Later, they did compete against Utah and the SEC schools, like Alabama, Auburn, Florida, Georgia, and LSU. Unfortunately, they never won any big conference championships.

She continued to spend her summers at Camp Tsukara for two years during the summer while in college. Being a counselor was way more fun than being a camper. Mark Diab and Mari-Rae served part of their time as staff members in the camp store. "Hey, Mari-Rae," said Mark, looking over the books. "Check this out. This kid has over $300 in his account. Want to grab a few candy bars on him?"

Mari-Rae's eyebrows shot up and her jaw dropped open. "Oh, no you don't!" She wagged an accusing finger in his face. "His parents gave him that money for his own use, not for us to pilfer."

"Hell, you know damn well the counselors grabbed things on us all the time when we were campers."

Mari-Rae was aghast. Her eyes got as big as saucers. "No. Oh, no you don't!" She shook a finger at Mark. "That is not our money. Don't you dare touch it!" No one was going to pull any stunts like that on her watch.

"Okay, okay. Sheesh." Mark shook his head and walked away.

"Mari-Rae immediately became my idol," said Deb Bryant (Janssen), when she first met Mari-Rae at Camp Tsukara. "She was so passionate and elegant." When Deb graduated high school a semester early, she headed straight for Iowa State so she could be around her idol. Mari-Rae took her under her wing and helped her with the transition into college gymnastics. "She was a perfectionist, sometimes to the detriment of herself and everyone around her," said Deb.

By this time, as an upper classman, Mari-Rae was a huge contributor to the team, offering suggestions on how to improve or add a degree of difficulty to raise their scores. She believed in them. It was always in good faith, wanting only the best for everyone. Mari-Rae never disrespected Coach, and together they all made a great team. She was voted Iowa State's Most Valuable Gymnast. By the time she graduated, the team was on its way. Thanks to Mari-Rae, future teams went up in ranking to second in the Big 8 Conference. They qualified at Regionals to compete in the National Championships and ended with a top twenty program in the nation. Excluding football and basketball, the gymnastics team pulled the highest crowds. Her attitude was key in changing the perception of Iowa State Gymnastics, both within their own team and the nation.

Mari-Rae reached out to both her coaches for advice. Coach Mike told her that with her fantastic memory she should go to law school. Law school? No way. She'd find a job coaching somewhere. When she was home on break she sought out Coach P from Fremd High School.

"How about some sushi?" she asked her old friend.

"Sure," said Coach P. "And I'll introduce you to my new team. They'll be so psyched to meet you."

Mari-Rae waved her hand in the air as she spoke. "P, what do you think I should do? I'm almost ready to graduate. I see nothing on the horizon. What about my dream to be a collegiate coach?"

Coach Petrillo smiled at her. "Mari-Rae, the one thing I know about you is you will never give up. If that is what you want, you'll get it. Trust me."

Mari-Rae came home for a short break. She didn't stay for the graduation ceremony. She just had no interest in it. She could have attended, but she would have only received a blank piece of paper until she finished the internship requirement for graduation. Instead, she loaded up her car and went home to Illinois. She did her internship at a local health club and earned her degree in Exercise Science. The year was 1988 and she once again threw herself into politics. Bill Clinton was picked to give the nominating speech for Michael Dukakis. Mari-Rae was enthralled with Clinton. It made for great debates over beers at the local pub.

"You've got to be kidding," one of her friends chided. "Did you listen to that speech? Boring."

The Party saw the blunder, too. They quickly got Clinton an appearance on the Johnny Carson show. Clinton poked fun at his own blunder and, with the flair of the next American Camelot, redeemed himself.

The summer was over. She was a college graduate. What now? She discussed it with her friends, with Coach Mike and Coach P. The International Gymnastic Magazine had a classified section. She couldn't believe her eyes. An ad asked for a gymnastics coach at a private club. A professional coaching job–in Dallas, Texas. She made the phone call and mailed her resume. Even she thought it was quite impressive for her age. Granted, she was no Béla Károlyi, but with the salary they were offering, they weren't expecting that. She accepted the job.

Mari-Rae Sopper - born June 19, 1966

with Mom, Marion

with Dad, Bill

with new baby sister

sisters   home on Hudson

Sopper / Kminek wedding   Dahlstrom farm

school pictures

home on Canterbury

Palatine Park District 1979

Within Her Grasp

Camp Tsukara

63

Within Her Grasp

Fremd High School

Iowa State University

Within Her Grasp

North Texas University

Dallas condo   Mari-Rae and Luther

photo shoot

Within Her Grasp

University of Denver

Denver home on Rosemary

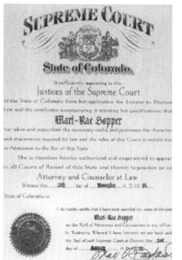

Sturm College of Law
Juris Doctorate
May 18, 1996

Within Her Grasp

United States Navy Jag Corps

Annapolis condo

Within Her Grasp

Remembering good times

Iowa State Gymnastics Reunion
2000

bridal shower celebration

D.C. condo on Kalorama

Sammy the cat

Memories

Grandma and Grandpa Dahlstrom, Mari-Rae and Lynn

Camp Tsukara Reunion 2001   Sisters in dance

Within Her Grasp

September 11, 2001

Arlington Cemetery | Mari-Rae's bench

5 North Texas University - It's a Long Road

"Mari-Rae's zest for life greatly impacted everyone around her. She set a great example for how we should live our lives and love our families and friends."
Stephanie Riska Pearson

The summer of 1988, off to Texas she went. Marion and Mari-Rae took turns driving from Illinois to the Dallas-Fort Worth area. With Marion's help, they found a foreclosed property and put an offer on it. But her income was not enough to qualify for the mortgage. She got a second job as a personal trainer in a health club. She needed a couple weeks' pay stubs to qualify and the bank wouldn't let her move in before closing. The real estate agent found a place for her to rent a room for a few weeks. By early fall, she was settled into her condo.

Working two jobs filled up most of her time, but she was happy and called home a lot to tell all about her coaching job. She met a guy, and for a while, things were terrific. Then, caught up in the happiness of a job she loved and a guy she was falling for, she repeated her old pattern with men. She told him her plan. In her mind, it was so simple; where they would live, how their life together would be wonderful. He bolted, just like all of the others.

"What's wrong with me?" Mari-Rae cried into the phone to her mother. "Why am I never 'the one' for someone? Don't I deserve to be loved?"

Marion's heart broke for her daughter. The pattern was always the same. Mari-Rae came on too strong; she scared them away. She tried to explain that men worked at different paces than women; that she had to be patient and let them decide when they were ready for the next step.

Mari-Rae followed him, begging him to come back, wanting to understand what she did wrong. Finally, he filed a restraining order against her.

The phone rang at Marion's house in Illinois. She could tell right away something was wrong. Mari-Rae was crying and very upset and her words were slurring. Marion managed to get out of her that it had something to do with this guy she'd been dating.

"Mari-Rae," her mother said. "What have you taken?"

She wouldn't say and hung up.

It was obvious that she was in some sort of distress. Panicked, Marion called 9-1-1 in Dallas. The EMTs went to her condo and took her to the hospital. She had overdosed on sleeping pills. They pumped her stomach.

Later, Mari-Rae claimed that she only wanted to go to sleep, that it wasn't a suicide attempt. Marion was not convinced. She had seen her deep falls into depression before.

Frank, her step-father sent her a letter. Despite their ability to bring out the worst in each other, he loved her. The letter read, "I'll be there for you no matter what. Do you need me to come there?" Mari-Rae never answered or acknowledged the letter.

Maybe she'd go back to college, get her Master's degree so she could be a collegiate coach. She did her research. North Texas University in Dallas had a good Master's program. She'd get her MS in Athletic Administration. Then she could move on to bigger and better things. She enrolled in North Texas and took night classes so she could continue to work. For a year, she was the Junior Olympic gymnastics coach.

It was an election year and Mari-Rae delved in head first. A die-hard Democrat, she'd corner her friends most Fridays at their local weekend hang-out, the Ginger Man. It was a diverse crowd, with up-and-coming attorneys from big Dallas corporate law firms drinking martinis, and health fanatics drinking eucalyptus water. Mari-Rae sipped on a beer, often talking so much that one glass would last for hours. Most shared her liberal beliefs, as a large majority of the suits were gay. She was clearly socially minded. If you happened to be from the other side of the aisle, you could expect a friendly confrontation from Mari-Rae.

"You want to put Bush back in office? Are you insane? The Republicans closed the publicly funded mental institutions. They put all those people out on the streets. Of course, if you are a social worker or in the mental health field, I guess that's job security," Mari-Rae waved her arms as she spoke, brushing her hair out of her eyes every few sentences. She proudly sported a "Rock the Vote" button, MTV's campaign to get young people to register to vote.

"But what about national security? Bush has a handle on the Middle East."

"No way," Mari-Rae said. "He's driving us into a war we don't want and don't need."

Her eyes widened into blue-green pools of glass. "This isn't your Dad's election," she quoted from Clinton's campaign mantra. "It's time for fresh blood, someone with a real pulse on what is happening. Clinton is the 'New Democrat.'"[6]

She sold her condo and moved into an apartment. She was not convinced that Dallas was the place for her and wanted to be able to move quickly if the right opportunity appeared. The apartment was horrible. Something triggered her allergies and she could never get comfortable.

The job as the coach came to an end in 1992. The attendance was down; they had to cut back. Not a personal reflection on her, but last in, first out. She took a telemarketing job with a start-up marketing company for the performing arts, selling season tickets. Four women started at the same time, Mari-Rae, Beth Geisler (Singel), Stephanie Riska (Pearson), and an older woman. The three young girls immediately hit it off. It was a horrible job. They thought their boss was some sort of shyster. The girls could only do so much marketing to people who didn't want what they were selling. By the end of October, they all needed a night on the town. Mari-Rae, Stephanie, and Beth headed out for a Halloween party. The girls dressed as the Three Blind Mice and headed to the party hosted by some friends.

A blind mouse couldn't see, right? Mari-Rae took to the part like she was born sightless. Stephanie and Beth peeked from behind dark glasses to find their way

---

[6] A Life in Brief Campaigns and Elections Copyright©2015 Rector and Visitors of the University of Virginia

through the maze of college bodies and sticky beer-coated floors. If Mari-Rae ever peeked through those dark glasses, no one could tell. She stumbled into rooms, pawed her way down the hallways, bumped into fellow revelers. She reached to the left when someone handed her a drink on the right. It was hysterical, and she was the life of the party.

After that job, she worked at a fitness gym selling memberships. Hard-core sales was really not her thing.

One particular Friday night, she was the designated driver to the Ginger Man. It was almost election time. The debate between incumbent President George H.W. Bush, Ross Perot, and Bill Clinton had aired on Sunday, October 11, 1992[7]. Beth and her friend, Annette Hunt, were on the opposing side—Republicans, set on voting for Bush. Mari-Rae commanded the room with her auditory on the benefits of voting for Bill Clinton.

Mari-Rae pulled into the parking garage of Annette's apartment. She was still in deep debate and not ready to give up, even when everyone else had given up arguing. "Please, God, whatever you do, don't vote for George Bush. It's a rich old boys' club."

Annette reached for the door. She'd heard enough for the last four hours. It was all Mari-Rae had talked about. Click. "What?" Annette stared at her friend. "You're locking us in?" Incredible.

Mari-Rae wasn't finished with her campaign. For forty-five minutes, she quoted every word from the debate verbatim. Her memory for details was astounding.

---

[7] Life Before the Presidency Domestic Affairs Copyright©2015 Rector and Visitors of the University of Virginia

"The Reagan-Bush administration put us in a three hundred billion dollar deficit. Do you ever want a real job, not telemarketing services nobody wants? Well, thanks to them, you may be doing that until you're eighty, unless you are on the unemployment line. Clinton's on *your* side, the side of the little guy. He's all about jobs, law and order, and personal responsibility."

"Clinton was a draft dodger. He used his Rhodes scholarship to get him out of the country so he wouldn't be drafted."

"Not so," said Mari-Rae. "He put himself right back into the lottery when he got back from England."

"Sure, *after* he was sure to end up with a high number. He never served in the military. How can he ever be Commander-in-Chief? He's clueless how to lead the world's largest military force."

"We don't *need* or want a big military force," Mari-Rae sputtered. "We should be taking care of our own people, not be the whole world's keeper."

"Let us out of the car, Mari-Rae," Annette pleaded. "You can't hold us captive until we change our vote."

Finally, reluctantly, the child locks came off and they were able to escape. The Clinton/Gore campaign won out and William B. Clinton was voted into the office of the Presidency in 1992 at the young age of forty-six, the third youngest president, and the first from the baby-boomer generation.

Beth introduced Mari-Rae to Nick. A few years older and out of school, working for an architectural firm, Nick made her happy. It was casual and relaxed. For perhaps the first time in her life, she was truly happy. The highs and lows of her mania vanished. Perhaps the doctors had put her on medication after the overdose incident. Perhaps it was Nick. Had she finally learned to let a relationship take its own course? No one knows. But she was relaxed, enjoying the company of a man without sabotaging the relationship. School was almost over and, other than finals, it was clear sailing.

A group of twenty rented a conversion van and went together to the Jimmy Buffet concert at Starbox Amphitheater in Dallas. There wasn't enough room for everyone so Mari-Rae sat on Nick's lap. "I didn't mind a bit," laughed Nick. "She was darling and a tiny little thing,"

She received her MS in Athletic Administration in the spring of 1993. Mari-Rae was ready to go after her dream job–as a collegiate gymnastics coach. She knew everybody in the gymnastics community, not just locally, but nationwide. A virtual memory bank of information, she knew every coach, every gymnast with any chance in collegiate or Olympic competition. She knew the rule book like the back of her hand. Schools should have been clamoring to bring her on board. The airwaves were as silent as a stealth bomber. Where were all the schools needing coaches? There had to be openings somewhere.

Mari-Rae tackled job hunting like she did everything else. No one was hiring. What was she going to do? Six years of higher education, her focus clear and defined, it should have been falling into place. Nothing. But the gymnastics buzz was fading and the program was being dropped by colleges all over the county.

She talked to her old friends. "You could go into law," Coach Sharples, from Iowa State, said during one of their many phone conversations. He had mentioned this to her once before, after Iowa State, but then she wasn't receptive to hear it. Times have changed.

"But…what would I do there?" The idea did have some intrigue.

"Sports law. With your keen ability to remember facts, you could do a great job representing athletes. Help them with their professional team contracts, endorsements, erroneous allegations, which always pop up with athletes. You'd be terrific."

Mari-Rae wasn't sure. Things looked farther and farther away from her dream.

Nick and Mari-Rae said goodbye as she headed off to law school in Denver. It was sad parting, but they promised to stay in touch. He had been a calming force and a bright spot in her otherwise tumultuous life.

6 University of Denver – Change in Focus

"She was driven by competitive excellence. Mari-Rae elevated the sport to an art form."   Ennis Hudson, *Colorado Gymnastic Institute*

A new school. A new direction. The University of Denver had a great law program. Mari-Rae applied and was easily accepted into the Sturm College of Law.

The scenery in Denver was different from Dallas. Unlike the flat topography around Dallas, the Rocky Mountains loomed large and majestic around the town. In August of 1993, when she first set foot on the Sturm College campus at the University of Denver, the trees were already turning colors, and in spite of the three hundred days of sunshine promised, the air was thin and crisp in the mile-high city. It played havoc with her breathing. She'd acclimate. She had no choice.

The campus was beautiful and the building for the Sturm law school was majestic. Up the granite steps, three large archways enclosed the double doors and windows. Above the doorway, gold letters spelled out *Sturm College of Law*. Red metal railings encircled an elevated courtyard with matching red iron tables and chairs. Sturm College was at the end of a cul-de-sac with a brick paved circle; colorful orange and red flowers filled the circle. This was a place where she could enjoy studying.

The real estate market was hot, so with Marion's help, and the FHA allowing parents to assist in their child's housing, Mari-Rae bought a little house sight unseen on Rosemary Street about seven miles from the university. Another law student roomed with her for a while and helped with the mortgage payments. Mari-Rae learned early on the benefits of home ownership.

She also brought Luther, her cat, from Dallas. Luther was cute, with a black mask and black-and-white paws, but Mari-Rae's allergies went crazy. Her nose ran and her eyes swelled almost shut until she got some allergy medicine, but she wouldn't give up Luther. She washed her hands constantly, thinking the allergy would be less if she didn't touch Luther. Not exactly a match made in heaven.

She put her nose to the grindstone and concentrated on her goal, a career in Athletic Law. She was tenacious in class. With law, everything is debatable, the Socratic method of teaching, and Mari-Rae knew how to debate. When other students slunk in their seats, hoping the professor wouldn't call on them. Mari-Rae could always be found frantically waving her hand in the air. The deeper turn the subject took, the more animated she'd become. This method of teaching taught students to think on their feet, and Mari-Rae excelled.[8]

Mari-Rae didn't forget her passion for gymnastics. She worked as a graduate assistant at the University of Denver Women's Gymnastics team for one year, and then she walked into the Colorado Gymnastics

---

[8] From Conn Flanigan, Sturm Law School, Mari-Rae Memorial Site

Institute in Aurora, Colorado. She asked Lindy Franzini-Carpenter, the owner, for a job working nights when she wasn't in school.

At first, Mari-Rae shadowed Coach Ennis Hudson at Colorado Gymnastics Institute. It wasn't long before the staff could see the gem they had in Mari-Rae. Ennis said of his first impression meeting her. "She impressed the hell out of us with her personality. She had a spark in her eyes and was so articulate."

She worked with the girls on dance for their compulsory routines, and later doing the choreography for the older girls for their optionals. "Some coaches come in with a big ego," said Ennis. "They could teach the mechanics of gymnastics from A-Z, but Mari-Rae was different. She had that spark in her eyes. CGI is a premier competitive program and we all rely on each other. She instantly fit in. She was driven by competitive excellence. Mari-Rae elevated the sport to an art form."

Andrea McGary was one of the girls whom Mari-Rae coached. She went on to attend Temple University. "I won the Mari-Rae Spirit Award at Temple University," said Andrea. "Little did they know that Mari-Rae was my first choreographer at Colorado Gymnastics Institute. It was an honor I cherish today." [9]

Mari-Rae was driven to find the best in each gymnast, but every gymnast was not a success story. When that happened, Mari-Rae took it personally, pushing her to a dark place. She had failed them. Their shortcomings were her failures.

After a rigorous schedule of school and work, Mari-Rae occasionally accepted invitations from Lindy and the other instructors to hit the bars in Denver for a

[9] From the Mari-Rae Sopper Memorial Website

few drinks and relaxation. "She came out with us for New Year's Eve," said Lindy. It was a great time. Mari-Rae was always smiling and easy to get along with. Mari-Rae brightened every room she walked into.[10]

Sometimes she and Ennis would track down the local sushi bar. The talk ultimately turned to gymnasts, how they could improve their performances. Casual friends, sometimes they hiked together in Boulder. "She was never driven by money. Helping the other gymnasts or fighting for what she deemed as righteous or just was much more important to her. She took her studying seriously and kept to herself a lot," said Ennis.

Most of the time, Mari-Rae had successfully hidden her manic-depressive personality.

The Sturm Law School was close to the Crimson and Gold Tavern on University Blvd and became a frequent watering hole for Mari-Rae and her friends. With no Dairy Queen in site, Mari-Rae had to substitute her DQ Blizzard from Iowa State days with a Sunday treat at the local Ben & Jerry's on Evans Avenue.

Mari-Rae met Jennifer Rudy (Bannon) who was visiting with another friend from the University of Denver. "She was the best choreographer I had ever seen," said Jennifer. She would turn out to be one of Mari-Rae's "forever" friends who would ultimately be one of the key players in Mari-Rae fulfilling her dream.

Mari-Rae spent many Friday lunches at the local sushi restaurant along with good friends, Sandy Jamison and their other friends, Kathleen, Lia, and Theresa. Mari-Rae entertained them with her latest romantic interests.

---

[10] Deanna Nino, Mari-Rae Memorial Site

"Was calling his house three times a day too much? Why didn't he invite me to meet his parents? Was he trying to hide something?"

She was so intense that it became laughable.

"Relax, Mari-Rae. You can't pounce on men that like," Sandy said.

If she wasn't strategizing her next move with her latest flame, she was defending the underdog on one political issue after another. The other girls were more laid back, so Mari-Rae's antics were the entertainment for the day. She talked non-stop, fixating on every small detail, whether it was a man or a political topic.

Mari-Rae competed in 5Ks, charity event runs, and 10K runs. Always in great shape, she and Sandy became steady running partners. Mari-Rae had her routines. Same routes, same number of miles, always even numbers.

During her more reflective moods, she discussed other pressing issues. Was athletic law really where she wanted to be? Where were the athletes that needed representation? Did she want to stay in Denver? What other options did she have?

As high as her successes in gymnastics had taken her, the deeper it plunged her into depression over her current jobless situation. Her student loans were stacking up against her. She was only six months away from finishing school and taking the bar. There was nothing available in athletic law as she had planned. She reached out to the athletic community but everything resulted with a dead end. First pursuing gymnastic athletes to no avail, she branched out to any professional athlete. There were certainly plenty of those in Denver, but nobody needed her representation.

She interviewed with a few judges in town, but they didn't pan out. A judge from a neighboring state was interested in interviewing her. She was tired and stressed. The interview did not go well. Grumbling under her breath, she just wanted to get home and curl up under the covers. On her way home, a semi-truck lost its treads two cars ahead of her. The car directly in front of her managed to miss the rubber debris. Tired, her reaction time was slow. She swerved and lost control of the car. In five seconds that felt like slow motion, she spun off the road and into a ditch, upside down. Her heart pounded out of her chest. The sound of other cars whizzing by, above the ditch, sounded like they were coming right at her. She hung there upside down, blood and adrenaline rushing to her head.

Voices of bystanders echoed in her ears. "Are you okay? We've called 9-1-1. Don't move."

She smelled gas. What if the car exploded with her stuck inside? She had to get out. Was she hurt? Could she move? No, Yes. She wasn't hurt and, yes, she could move. She unhooked her seatbelt, righted herself from her inverted position and crawled to the back. The rear window of the hatchback had broken out. She pulled herself to safety.

The police arrived. No, she wasn't hurt. No, she didn't need an ambulance. She didn't want to pay for it. After an extended argument, the officer drove her to a gas station and left her there.

Standing at a pay phone, she tried all her friends. No one was answering their phones. What should she do? She was running out of change. How would she get home? Finally, she got through to a friend. "What's up?"

"I have some good news and some bad news," said Mari-Rae.

Mari-Rae asked her mother for help applying for an internship. Marion put out her feelers in her community. A friend's step-father was Justice Stevens, but when Marion told Mari-Rae, she didn't believe her and wouldn't follow through. After much convincing, Mari-Rae gave her résumé to her mother to pass along, which she did. It didn't help. There would be no internship.

Her good friend, Sandy Jamison had enlisted in the Navy six months earlier.

"What do you think? Do you think it is for me?" Mari-Rae asked Sandy.

"Talk to a recruiter," encouraged Sandy. "Talk to several. Just because I chose the Navy doesn't mean it's right for you."

Mari-Rae talked to all of the military recruiters. She made lists. She examined the pros and cons. Her living room was lined with dry erase boards. The idea of defending a young soldier or sailor against the "establishment" appealed to her. Pro list. But did she want to become part of the establishment? Con list. It wasn't that she wasn't patriotic. She was abundantly so. Yes, she wanted to fight for justice. She decided to follow in her friend's footsteps. It was settled. She'd join the Navy. New goal, new path.

She filled out all of the paperwork, mounds of personal information, submitted school transcripts, obtained recommendations, passed her physical with flying colors.

Excited about having another clear goal once again, she was thrilled when she received her acceptance letter in the mail the same day the Navy recruiter called her with the news.

She graduated with her Juris Doctorate on May 18, 1996. Her mother, step-father, Frank, father, Bill, were there to see her graduate. So excited about graduating, she had forgotten to eat when her parents picked her up at home. Denver was beautiful in May and the ceremony was held outside. By the time they got to "S" for Sopper, Mari-Rae was wilting. Sugar crashes were nothing new to her. She was dizzy and weak. If she could just make it off the platform, she could get something to eat. She smiled at the audience as she accepted her diploma. Please, let this be over so she could get something to eat. People wanted to linger and chat, to congratulate the graduates. Mari-Rae wanted to get to the small reception where there was food. She brushed off people's congratulations. They needed to go, now. Along the way, her mother, Marion, spotted a bank of pay phones. Her pager had been going off through the ceremony. Like any successful real estate agent, she had to make the call back. Everyone waited. One call turned into two. Mari-Rae couldn't believe it. Why did she have to make the call now? She didn't do it during her sister's wedding.

"No," Marion replied. "But I did during the rehearsal dinner. Besides, I waited until after the graduation ceremony."

That was it. Mari-Rae was leaving without the lot of them. They could find their own way to the reception. She was going to get some food.

During her parents' stay in Denver, Mari-Rae played tour director. Back to herself with a full stomach, she showed them all around the area. It had turned out to be a wonderful place to live, full of healthy people, sunshine, mountains and friends. Prices had gone up on real estate since she bought her home. She would make a nice profit.

She took the Colorado Bar and passed it the first time. She had her new plan.

Mari-Rae's mind worked at a different speed than most, and often with strange results. The girls planned a Fourth of July barbecue. They met up at the sushi restaurant to plan the event.

"I'll bring the burgers and hot dogs," said Sandy.

"I'll bring a cooler and the beer," chimed in Kathleen.

Lia nodded between bites. "Put me down for coleslaw and potato salad. What are you bringing Mari-Rae?"

"Lasagna... I'll bring lasagna."

The girls looked at each other? Lasagna? In 80 degree weather at a barbecue? To each her own. And she did. She showed up with several trays of lasagna – which later became the stand-in joke about hot-weather food.

It was time to leave. She'd make the trek from Denver to Baltimore alone. Her townhome in Annapolis was ready for her. She had bought it when she flew there earlier in the year. The large things had been shipped. Her car was loaded with small items and just enough room for her and Luther. Where was Luther? She searched the house. Nowhere to be found. The movers and the excitement had forced him into seclusion. Finally, Mari-Rae found him in a hole in the wall under the kitchen sink. Seriously, Luther? Now. She didn't need this. She coaxed. His beady eyes stared out at her but he wouldn't budge. He was far enough back that she couldn't reach him, even with the contortions she went through to fit under the sink and see into the hole. Should she just leave him? Coax a little more. "Seriously, Luther, I'm going to leave you." She crawled out from under the sink. Could she really do it? Just leave him there? As she contemplated, sitting on the floor, leaning against the cabinets, two little ears came into view. Then a head. He was out!

She scooped him up and shoved him into the crate, not too gently. He didn't like it. She didn't care at this point. She needed to get on the road. She made it as far as Oskaloosa, Iowa, and spent the night with her step-brother, Frank, his wife Beth, and their family. The second night, she made it as far as her mother's home in Illinois. She left Luther with them while in OCS, Officer Candidate School.

7   United States Navy JAG – Justice for All

Mari-Rae made the Navy a better place. She brought honor, integrity, and courage to every case she ever had, and she fought hard for every client she represented."
Jennifer Eichenmuller

By the time Mari-Rae arrived at her parents' house, Luther was a mess. He had rubbed off all his whiskers because he had been confined so long in the cage. The first time Frank tried to pet him, Luther bit him. With persistence, Frank earned Luther's trust and they became fast friends. By the time she was done with her training, Luther would have nothing to do with Mari-Rae. Frank had just adopted a cat.

There was six weeks of Navy legal training, a short break, then nine more weeks, including court martial training.

Mari-Rae reunited with Sandy Jamison from Denver Law School at OCS in Newport, Rhode Island. They were in different schools, but would be later assigned to Washington D.C. at the same time. "She was fun to be around," said Sandy. "A really funny person, talking non-stop, fixating on every tiny detail of her life."

"Sometimes we would go down to Newport Beach," said Sandy. Mari-Rae would be down on the beach in her bikini doing hand springs and other gymnastic stunts. "Of course, none of the rest of us could do them, or would be caught dead in a skimpy bikini."

Mari-Rae was already at the local sushi bar when they joined her. "Just look at this hemline!" Mari-Rae squealed, not too quietly. "I can't wear this. It makes my calves look fat." A bowl of rice was already in front of her. "Sorry, I didn't wait for you to order. I'm starving."

Sandy dropped in the booth across from her, smiling to herself. *You're ALWAYS starving.* "I don't think that's optional," Sandy said. Mari-Rae always made her laugh and she couldn't think about her without laughing. Mari-Rae said or did the craziest things.

With all of Mari-Rae's spontaneity, there were certain things her family and friends could always count on with Mari-Rae. She loved sushi, was a health nut, always hungry, always passionate, always waving her hand as she spoke, emphasizing her point. She was really quite predictable. She also had a rare quality of always seeing the best in everyone. She was never judgmental, even when she disagreed with you.

"Who do I need to contact? I'll get this fixed." Mari-Rae insisted.

Change Navy protocol for one cadet? Not likely.

Mari-Rae took on 'Operation Hemline' as a high priority. If she could just explain to a reasonable officer that two inches would make all the difference in the world, she was sure to get her way.

Sandy knew she was preaching to the choir but she had to give Mari-Rae credit for taking on "the establishment." But it wasn't only the hemline, it was hair clips, and the sweater, standard issue, but not authorized to wear to class.

Exasperated, Mari-Rae reasoned. "Well they issued it to us. Why would they do that if I can't wear it?"

Good point, but not one she would win.

Her other friend, Linda Bowers watched Mari-Rae break down and cry over the sweater debacle. "She was cold," said Linda. "And she couldn't understand why they wouldn't reason with her. I felt so bad."

Mari-Rae was convinced that nobody noticed her six inch banana clip pinned in her hair while the other cadets obediently wore the Navy approved Goody barrettes. If anyone ever could adjust their uniform to fit their wants or perceived needs, it was Mari-Rae.

When OCS ended, she spent three weeks in Norfolk, Virginia, on a Navy vessel. This wasn't legal training. It was put-yourself-in-their-shoes training so she could get a taste of a true sailor's life.

It was 1996, and Mari-Rae had purchased a new condo in Annapolis, Maryland, when she still lived in Denver. It was ready for her when she finished her training. They said she'd be assigned there. A review board monitored her for six months for fitness determination before giving her the official assignment.

In true Mari-Rae style, she was very opinionated about people commuting more than ten miles. They must be out of their minds. "I'd never do that," she told her mother. You know what they say: "Never say never."

She passed the fitness determination and orders changed. She was assigned to the Naval Ship Yard in Washington, D.C., forty miles away from her condo. An hour drive in good traffic, but Maryland/D.C. traffic was predictably a traffic jam, and the commute could be twice that long. She couldn't up and sell her condo without taking a bath. She had no choice. The dreaded commute. With her sincere desire for punctuality, but propensity for always being late, she couldn't take any chances on traffic and routinely left for work every day two-and-a-half hours before her scheduled time.

Mari-Rae met Jennifer Rankin when she was visiting her good friend, Joe Edgell, in Seattle. Jennifer had just finished grad school and was on a cross-country trek. Mari-Rae was on a high and talked non-stop to Jennifer. "Look me up if you ever get to D.C." she said.

Jennifer thought it was a courteous platitude until, months later, Mari-Rae followed up with her, checking on how her cross-country trip was going. The trek had been great; surprise, Jennifer was going to make it to D.C. after all. She would be there for a few months with a job assignment.

True to her word, as soon as Jennifer was settled, Mari-Rae was there as the welcoming party. She made sure that Jennifer went with her to all of the parties in town, that she met Mari-Rae's friends, and that she was never alone. Mari-Rae and Jennifer even attended a viewing party for the University of Texas—Iowa State Football game. "She took on a bar full of UT fans, chin first," said Jennifer. "She was a bright spot in an otherwise dreary six-month stay in D.C."[11]

The Navy Legal Service Office was difficult for Mari-Rae. Why was it so difficult to separate her strong personal beliefs in fairness and right and wrong with the hard and fast unquestionable Navy legal system? Emotions peaked and valleyed like a roller coaster. This was a mistake. No, she could do this. *Say it, Mari-Rae.*

---

[11] Jennifer Rankin, Mari-Rae Memorial Site

You can do this. The system just wasn't fair to her clients. Maybe she wasn't cut out for Navy life.

In 1997, Jennifer Eichenmuller's supervisor issued her an ultimatum. They could transfer Mari-Rae to Appellate Defense or they would have to give her a medical discharge. Mari-Rae just wasn't fitting into the Navy Legal Service. She lost it in the court room, getting very emotional, and tears streaming down her face. In Mari-Rae's defense, Navy law was a hard place to work, a sexist environment, primarily a man's domain. It was acceptable for the male officers to use profanity, to make sexual innuendos toward the female officers, but it wasn't okay to cry in the courtroom.

Navy docs diagnosed her as bi-polar. Finally, there was an answer to the whirlwind of emotions she went through. It was liberating to have a tangible name for it–bi-polar. Scenes from her life flashed by like clips from movies. The mania, when everything was right with the world, when she could do no wrong, do nothing but succeed. The plan was decisive and clear. She lived much of her life through her plans. Then there was the depression, when nobody understood her, when she felt abandoned and alone. Nobody would ever truly love her. She was a failure.

Ahh! Like a lightbulb going off in her head, it all made sense. The doc said it could be controlled. There was medication. She'd been there before, after the suicide attempt. She'd tried anti-depressants. They made her foggy and unable to function. She fought the idea of being medicated. Navy doctors don't give suggestions, they give orders. They put her on Lithium, a different drug from the antidepressants. The moods evened out. The highs were not as high, or as decisive, but the lows were manageable. It was imperative that she stay on her meds.

Jennifer accepted the challenge. It would be a shame for a talented lawyer like Mari-Rae to be discharged before she could prove herself. She saw the potential, the passion in Mari-Rae. Appellate Defense was one of those rare departments where it was good to question authority in order to get justice for the client. Many still cowered to the pressures of the status quo. Not Mari-Rae. She challenged her coworkers to think independently and decide what was best for their clients and not what best for the Navy

Mari-Rae loved appellate defense. She was ferocious when defending her clients and ideals. It didn't take long for her and Jennifer to become good friends. They had to stick together in the male-dominated environment.

"These guys are tough," Jennifer would say to Mari-Rae. They'd lock themselves in one of their offices to vent and lean on each other for support. Somehow, Jennifer would find a way to make Mari-Rae laugh through her tears, square her shoulders and face another day.

In the cafeteria, it was easy to spot Mari-Rae before you could actually see her small frame among the brawny men. They guys liked to rile her up, which wasn't hard to do. Her voice carried across the room, loudly defending her side in the debate, one hand pounding the table, the other waving a veggie patty on a bun, her eyes wide with excitement, her face getting redder by the minute.

When Mari-Rae wasn't defending the underdog, she was volunteering her time. Women's and children's rights ranked high on her list. In spite of her extremely large case-load, she took a couple of hours every week to mentor an at-risk child from a very poor section of Alexandria, Virginia, even if it meant working nights or weekends to catch up.

Mari-Rae was irreverent to her superiors. She had ideas that didn't fit into the "box." Some people thought she didn't belong in the military. What if they were wrong? What if she was exactly what the Navy needed as an Appellate lawyer to defend her client? They could always count on her honest opinion, grounded in her research and guarding her cause to the end.

For those who ever posed that question, "Is the Navy ready for Mari-Rae?" said Jennifer, "I have the answer. The Navy probably never had a more dedicated, passionate, intelligent lawyer. Mari-Rae made the Navy a better place. She brought honor, integrity, and courage to every case she ever had, and she fought hard for every client she represented."

She may have been a bit irreverent, but she was passionate.

Don Rehkopf mentored Mari-Rae on a case that was pending with the U.S. Supreme Court. He was the Co-Chair of the National Association of Criminal Defense Lawyers, Military Law Committee. He called her about a development in the case. It was Mari-Rae's opportunity to argue a case in the Supreme Court. Most attorneys would have jumped at the chance to have their moment in the spotlight. The problem was that it could jeopardize her client negatively. It wasn't in his best interest. Mari-Rae instantly knew that her actions would not only adversely affect this client, but set a precedent for future cases. It was not the right thing to do. "That case has had an impact on every death penalty case in the

United States, and also every military court-martial thereafter," said Mr. Rehkopf, Esquire.

Mari-Rae's high ideals always fought for justice, not the glory. She was an example to every other attorney not to let his client down. "Mari-Rae was always well-prepared, articulate, and forceful," said Andrew S. Effron, U.S. Court of Appeals Judge.[12]

Iowa State friend, Kathy Edwards Federico, frequently came to D.C. for her work in law enforcement. She had meetings at the FBI headquarters in Quantico. Mari-Rae never missed an opportunity to see her good friend. Mari-Rae had been a bridesmaid in her wedding in 1989. They went for lunch. Kathy had a burger, Mari-Rae a salad, with everything on the side.

Kathy looked down at Mari-Rae's ankle. "La-Mar, you have a tattoo! A dolphin?"

A dolphin? Was it her childhood memories of times on the beach with her sisters, or time training on the Navy ship that made her love dolphins? She never explained other than a shrug, "I like them. They're smart and they're free." It seemed like an unusual choice, but Mari-Rae was always full of surprises.

During one trip to D.C. with a delegation of U.S.–Saudi delegates from Zimbabwe. Sandy Jamison asked Mari-Rae if she would like to help escort the group around D.C., showing them the sites. Of course. Adorned in the dress blues, Sandy and Mari-Rae set out to show them the town. Their English was marginal and Mari-Rae flourished with hand motions and charades. They toured the Washington Monument, the Jefferson, and the Lincoln. They did the mini tour offered by the White House. They seemed most interested in the Pentagon. In

---

[12] Mari-Rae Sopper Memorial Site

the press briefing room, each delegate had their picture taken behind the podium, the Presidential seal in the background. When Mari-Rae took to the podium, she pretended she was the Secretary of Defense. A great photo of her behind the podium shows her glowing in the limelight.

After she left the Navy, Mari-Rae took a civilian job with a D.C. law firm that specialized in corporate law. She hated it with a passion. Not that they were doing anything wrong, but it wasn't her style of law. The job lasted less than a year. Was this all there was? What happened to her dream? She wanted so much out of life, to feel fulfilled, to be loved, to make a difference, to pursue her passion, gymnastics.

8 New Job, New City, New State, New Life

"She kept the values of our country close to heart."
Al Gore

"Mari-Rae helped me remember why I loved gymnastics.
Her willingness to make sacrifices to be part of a team
inspired me."....Jennifer Rudy Bannon

Mari-Rae decided that March of 2000 was a good year for an Iowa State University Gymnastics Reunion. She called Kathy Edwards Federico and started all the planning.

The day of the reunion arrived. Kathy and Debbie Diskerud Hatanpa were to pick up Mari-Rae at her hotel in Ames, Iowa. Mari-Rae wasn't ready and kept them waiting twenty minutes. Even after all those years, some things never changed.

When they got to the reunion, a photographer was taking pictures. Mari-Rae and Debbie were posing. The photographer took the photo landscape, getting a great close up of Debbie's long hair. Mari-Rae insisted on another shot, taken vertical, as a portrait with a full body shot. She wanted to show off her fit body.

So many great friends and memories from Iowa State. Debbie Diskerud Hatanpa, Sara Krause, Kathy

Edwards Federico, Lisa Salcedo, Shane Sanders and Jamie Goll. Many were married with children. Mari-Rae tamped down the tiny bit of jealousy that their love lives had worked out better than hers. She was truly happy for them. She regretted that Coach Mike Sharples, now living in North Carolina couldn't attend. She would have liked to see her good friend again.

2000 was also a good year for Mari-Rae to put on her political hat. Vice President Al Gore was running against George W. Bush for the Presidency. Gore didn't have the persona that his counterpart, Clinton, had and he bumbled his way through the debates. His main message was to attack George Bush. "Texas is number three in water pollution, number one in air pollution," Gore was quoted as saying. [13]

Deeply patriotic, she volunteered for the Democratic Party for the 2000 election.

Mari-Rae echoed the Gore warning about huge tax cuts for the wealthy if Republican George W. Bush was elected. She was on the political war path once again. Pennsylvania hung in the air as a swing vote that could make or break the election. Mari-Rae rallied all of her friends and colleagues to go with her to Pennsylvania to help with the campaign. She drove to Pennsylvania and went door-to-door handing out literature in support of the Gore/Lieberman ticket. Her convictions were mirrored in her enthusiasm. "She believed that an individual could make a difference in our democratic government. She made me believe that activism and

---

[13] Eric M. Appleman/Democracy in Action Copyright©2000, 2001

ideals really were not just meant to be the stuff of the youth," said Jennifer Eichenmuller.

One day, Mari-Rae bumped into George Stephanopoulos at a local dry cleaner in D.C. He was gorgeous, with thick brown hair and a strong jaw with a tiny cleft in his chin. An American television journalist and Democratic Party political advisor with a gilded tongue, he served as the de facto press secretary, briefing the press even though Dee Dee Myers was officially the press secretary during the Clinton administration. His memoir, *All Too Human: A Political Education,* which was on The New York Times Bestseller List, released after his resignation in 1999, sat on Mari-Rae's nightstand, dog-eared from reading and noting special lines.

She froze. For once in her life, she was tongue-tied. He smiled briefly at her, feeling her stare pierce into his head. *Say something*! Her mind was totally blank. He took his shirts and left. Damn. Should she follow him? Tell him that she was a fan? Before she could decide, he had disappeared down the street.

She told her friend, Sandy Jamison, all about it over sushi. "I blew it. He was right there. My mind went completely blank.

"You might see him again," her friend offered. "He's often seen around town in coffee shops and sushi restaurants. He must live here somewhere."

"Maybe I can accidently spill some coffee on him," Mari-Rae said. "He'd have to talk to me then. It would start a conversation."

Sandy laughed. "I wouldn't recommend that. Hot coffee in a man's lap is not exactly the best way to rope him in."

She shared the story with friend, Kathy Federico, over the phone. George sightings became a part of the game. Every time Mari-Rae would spot him around town, she'd call her friends to scheme how she could get to know him. "Did you know he's only five years older than me? That's perfect. We'd make beautiful children together. Can't you see them?"

She was relentless at both; following George Stephanopoulos and fighting for the campaign. "She kept the values of our country close to her heart . . ."said Al Gore. Unfortunately for Mari-Rae, and the Gore/Lieberman ticket, they were defeated in the November 2000 election, winning by popular vote, but losing by electoral votes to George W. Bush and Dick Cheney. But George Stephanopoulos was still on the loose.

Mari-Rae knew networking was the key to her claiming her future, and she knew lots of people. Her extraordinary memory for people and names would serve her well. For once, she was going to think about herself. Somewhere out there was a coaching job for her. It was April, 2001, and she headed to the NCAA nationals in Georgia. There were coaches from dozens of the top gymnastics programs and she was on a mission to find a job.

She booked her flight late and was at an obscure hotel a few miles away from the arena where the competition was taking place. She ran into Sandy Oldham from the Palatine High School and Palatine Park District gymnastics programs at the hotel pool. Sandy was judging the competition and trying to get some Georgia sunshine before the meets, thinking she was far enough away not to run into any students who were competing. She didn't want any suggestion that she had fraternized with any of the competitors.

"Mari-Rae," Sandy exclaimed. "What brings you here? Aren't you a big-shot attorney in D.C. now?"

Mari-Rae laughed. "Yep, but I'm here looking for a college coaching job. Everybody that is somebody is at this event. I'm determined to get some good leads, maybe even an offer."

"Good for you. You do realize that no coaching job is going to come close to the salary you're making now."

Mari-Rae nodded. "I know. But it's all I have ever wanted to do. I'd give up everything to be a head coach. When I was in Dallas, I coached the Junior Olympics team, and in Colorado, I choreographed for the Colorado Gymnastics Institute, and in Annapolis I also choreographed for the U.S. Naval Academy women's gymnastics team. In D.C., I volunteered for the George Washington University Gymnastics program to increase their attendance. Even parents in Dallas and other areas flew me to their gyms to personally choreograph their daughters' floor routines. And I did an internship at the Pan Am Games in Indianapolis working with Mike Jacki. Everywhere I have lived, I've stayed involved in gymnastics."

"You are a go-getter. It'll happen for you. I'll keep my eyes and ears open for you. If I hear of anything, I'll let you know."

Mari-Rae gave her a hug. "Thanks so much. It's so good to see you again."

Mike Jacki, from Camp Tsukara and USGF (United States Gymnastics Federation) was a terrific source for introductions. He introduced her to Paul Columbo, assistant coach at the University of Florida.

His winning personality made for easy conversation and they spent an entire evening talking.

"Why would you give up a well-paying job as an attorney to become a college coach? You're never going to get rich that way," Coach Columbo said.

"Because it's what I want to do," she responded. Didn't he understand? He was a coach, after all. Didn't every coach share that same burning desire? It was what she wanted more than anything in the world.

That night, Coach Columbo introduced Mari-Rae to some of the other coaches. Her passion was contagious. She passed out cards like candy, making sure everyone in the gymnastics world knew she was ready to make that leap. Some people patted her on the back saying, "Go for it and follow your dreams." But they had it wrong. Mari-Rae was never a follower. Mari-Rae was a leader. She was going after her dreams. She could feel it. She was not about to stop until she caught it.

Mari-Rae and Paul Columbo stayed in close touch. Every lead or tip Paul came across he forwarded to Mari-Rae. It was a great event and she walked away, stimulated, but without any offers.

In May, Mari-Rae gladly accepted an invitation for Sunday dinner in Silver Spring, Maryland, at Jennifer Eichenmuller's house. Jennifer was trying out a new Italian seafood stew because she knew Mari-Rae loved fish. It was met with some apathy and Jennifer promised to work on it if Mari-Rae would promise to visit her in Sicily where she was to be stationed in June. If anyone would keep her promise to visit, regardless of the miles, it was Mari-Rae. Mari-Rae never forgot a friend and she had an uncanny ability to keep in touch with the vast number of them from all over the globe.

When Kathy Edwards Federico came to D.C. for business, Mari-Rae always made time to spend with her. "She was loyal to the core," Kathy said. "She stood up for ideals, regardless of what anyone else thought."

Mari-Rae came home to Illinois the week of her thirty-fifth birthday, June, 2001. With the help of her father who previously lived in Bloomington, Illinois, she'd landed an interview with the Athletic Department at Illinois State University for the Head Coach position for their women's gymnastics team. She had the credentials and the education. She had a plan for the team. Still, she knew she didn't have the job before she walked out the door, even with their promise to keep her as a consideration. What went wrong? This was not the way to start her week.

That same week was the Tsukara Camp Reunion in the northwest Chicago suburbs. It was great to see all of her old friends, but a little sad to know the camp no longer existed. So many changes in the gymnastics community. She talked a mile a minute through the whole reunion, bouncing from friend to friend. "Mari-Rae, I think you have had enough caffeine!" her friends laughed. Mari-Rae didn't need caffeine. This was just Mari-Rae being Mari-Rae.

The day of her thirty-fifth birthday, June 19, Marion and Frank planned a cookout. Mari-Rae's Grandma Dahlstrom, her father, Bill Sopper, half-sister, Stacy, Uncle Kerry, step-brother Chris and her sister, Lynn were all there. But things were not falling into place for Mari-Rae. She was going to be thirty-five years old. When was her time for happiness? Those stupid pills weren't helping at all. She had previously thrown them down the toilet before leaving D.C. Everyone else was having a grand time. Mari-Rae spotted her sisters, Lynn and Stacy, whispering in the corner. Were they making fun of her? Were their lives that perfect that they could poke fun at her, a failure at thirty-five? She couldn't take it one more minute. Let them have their laugh. Mari-Rae lost it, screaming at them in front of everyone, and stormed into the house and up the stairs.

"What happened?" inquired Marion. "Did you girls say something to her?"

"No, we were just talking. We didn't even mention Mari-Rae. She's out of control," one of the girls said.

Marion sighed. "Lynn, it's her birthday. Go up and get her. Convince her that you weren't making fun of her. Don't ruin her day."

"We didn't ruin it," Lynn said. "She's the one making something out of nothing." Still, Lynn complied with their mother's request. She calmed Mari-Rae down and brought her back to the party.

Mari-Rae, without her meds, was an unpinned hand grenade.

Mari-Rae's position at Schmeltzer, Aptaker, and Shepard wasn't for her. The firm represented big corporations against the little guy plus it definitely was a "good ole boys club." It was the opposite of her philosophy. She was the defender of the underdog. She was so unhappy that by the beginning of August, she resigned. "Mari-Rae was a bright, very personable, and energetic young attorney. She was one that would have a bright future in whatever endeavor she decided to apply herself," said Ira Shepard, Esquire.

Some people might have considered her a pest, constantly calling and marketing herself to any college who would listen. She applied for each and every open coaching position, in addition to assistant coach positions. Tenacious in her pursuit, it became her full-time job until she received a call from Jennifer Rudy, senior team captain at UCSB (*University of California, Santa Barbara*). The head coach of UCSB, Megan Fenton, had retired at the end of Jennifer's junior year, and now, the assistant coach was also stepping down to open his own gym. Jennifer had received a call from Alice Henry in the Athletic Department.

"Who are the candidates for the position?" Jennifer asked.

Alice sent Jennifer a list of potential candidates. She immediately recognized Mari-Rae's name on the list. Jennifer remembered her from Colorado and she knew several gymnasts who were coached by Mari-Rae. She was perfect for the job.

Jennifer was in Washington D.C. interning at the Republican National Committee at the time. She called Mari-Rae. "Meet me at the little Mexican restaurant in the Adams Morgan district, and bring a copy of your resume."

Mari-Rae's heart skipped a beat. Could this be it? She couldn't get there fast enough. She slipped in the booth across from Jennifer. "What? I can't wait. Tell me the news."

Jennifer explained about the retiring coaches and how she had contacted the Athletic Department and told them that they must hire Mari-Rae. She looked over the resume, promising to forward it to Alice. Eventually, the talk turned to politics. The two girls couldn't have been on farther sides of the aisle, but their love for gymnastics gave them a special bond.

They talked nearly daily for hours. Both anxiously awaited the formal invitation. Jennifer forwarded Mari-Rae's resume and called the Athletic Department to see how things were going.

"I couldn't believe how much Mari-Rae already knew about our team," Jennifer told Alice. Mari-Rae had never met most of the girls but she knew all of their statistics. She knew whom to contact and what was needed to get it done. However, the news was not good. UCSB had decided to discontinue both the men's and women's gymnastics programs.

She called Mari-Rae with the bad news.

"Did I get the job?" This was it. Why hadn't they called her first?

"No," said Jennifer.

Mari-Rae's heart sunk. "They hired someone else?"

"Worse. They've decided to drop the gymnastic program altogether."

No, this couldn't happen. Mari-Rae's mind raced.

"It's so unfair," said Jennifer. "We don't have time to find another school with a gymnastics program. Nor will we be able to transfer our athletic scholarships."

"Wait," she said. "They can't do that. Tell them they have to extend the program." Instead of falling to defeat, Mari-Rae rose to the occasion. "I'll put together a prospectus. We'll build a campaign. We can't let the team down."

For four days, Jennifer and Mari-Rae made contacts, strategized, and brainstormed. "The battle felt like David and Goliath," said Jennifer.

Jennifer took their case to the Athletic Department. The program was re-instated.

Finally, Mari-Rae got the call. She had the job, but only for one year. The program still would be discontinued at the end of the year.

That's what they thought. They didn't know Mari-Rae. Jennifer and Mari-Rae celebrated the good news.

The idea that it would only be one year was not an acceptable solution to Mari-Rae. She pulled out all of the stops, leaning on every bit of experience, in the gym and in the courtroom, to build a case to save the program. For days she didn't sleep. Countless lists. A letter-writing campaign. Alumni–start with the alumni who were involved in gymnastics. Booster clubs. She pulled together a list. Get donations. Create a fund raiser. An invitational. Rally the team. Build their confidence. Her dream was an inch away. "I can do it," Mari-Rae exclaimed. "In two years, I'll have the program fully funded. Within five years, we'll be in the top ten." She believed every word of it.

"Mari-Rae," Jennifer said. "You are a breath of fresh air. I was losing my enthusiasm, but you've got me all psyched up for it again. You helped me remember why I love gymnastics."

They booked their flight together to fly back to UCSB together on September 11.

By the end of August, Mari-Rae had a workout routine and conditioning program to whip the girls into shape. It was rigorous and demanding.

"Yikes, I don't think I can do that." Jennifer told Mari-Rae, two weeks before they were to fly to California together. She was nowhere close to the physical condition that Mari-Rae was demanding. She hadn't worked out all summer.

Jennifer changed her flight to get back early on August 28 and start conditioning.

Mari-Rae had so much to do. Put the condo up for sale. Arrange movers. Pack. Say goodbye to her D.C. friends.

"Pinch me," Mari-Rae said into the phone. "Mom, I did it. I'm the head coach for UCSB. Can you believe it?"

"Of course you did it." Marion smiled into the receiver. "When haven't you accomplished what you went after?"

Mari-Rae called good friend, Stephanie Risko Pearson. "I'll call you as soon as I am settled in California." They talked about when Mari-Rae would next get a chance to see Stephanie in Texas and meet her new daughter, Sophia. They talked about all of the other people Mari-Rae wanted to see and all of the things she was going to do to turn the UCSB program around. Her excitement was contagious.

She sat down at her laptop and typed a group email to her family and closest friends. The subject line read, *New Job, New City, New State, New Life*." She had made it. It was all within her grasp, at last.

It was finally almost time. Mari-Rae looked around her apartment. She should be packing. Her car was going on the trailer on Friday. The movers were coming on Monday to pick up her things. There were still things hanging in her closet, pots and pans still in the cupboards.

Jennifer was going to keep Sammy, the cat, until Mari-Rae found a place in Santa Barbara. Until then, she would stay with another gymnast but cats weren't allowed in her building.

She hadn't always called home this often, but she just loved sharing her joy with everyone. "Mom, I know I should be packing, but Theresa Adams's bachelorette party is Friday night. And her wedding is on Saturday. Packing is taking more time than I planned. I've got so much to do but I'd hate to miss this."

"Go," said Marion. "This will be one of your last chances to see some of your friends. Go have some fun. It'll all get done."

Mari-Rae dressed in one her hottest outfits and met Sandy Jamison (Hodgkinson) and Kathleen Kelly to head out for the bachelorette party. She hadn't seen some of these girls from Denver University law school in years, everyone was scattered across the country.

Life was great. She was on top of the world. Stories bounced back and forth of old times. Mari-Rae danced to *I Will Survive* and *Da Butt*, singing along, *"Theresa's Got a Big Ol Butt, OhYeah"* in honor of the lovely bride. She beamed with happiness and excitement about her new job.

The wedding was perfect. Theresa looked beautiful. Would she ever get to wear a wedding gown? Not now. No time to sulk. She had a whole new life ahead of her.

Sunday morning she left a message on Sandy's voicemail. "I need you to come help me pack."

Sandy listened as Mari-Rae rambled on for about three minutes into the voice mail. Within a two-hour period, she had left two more similar messages.

"It's a typical Mari-Rae day." Sandy laughed to herself.

Sandy, her fiancé, Dave Hodgkinson, and another friend of Mari-Rae arrived on time, ready to pack her for the movers arriving the next morning.

Dave looked around at the stacks of things to pack. "Mari-Rae, where are all the boxes?"

There were no boxes, no packing material, and only a quarter roll of tape.

Mari-Rae shrugged. "I ran out." Typical.

Sandy and Dave did the best they could to wrap all of her pictures and valuables in towels, sheets, and blankets. Finally, Mari-Rae's sister, Christina, came to the rescue with a car load of boxes and tape.

That evening, her friends, Jim Bailey, Sandy, Dave, and another friend, planned a farewell party at Lauriol Plaza. The location was perfect, on 18th St. N.W., the rooftop restaurant was both a wonderful mix of white table elegance, with casual wood plank floors and ceilings, and a wall of windows from the rooftop dining room. It smelled heavenly. Rated one of the top Mexican restaurants in D.C., the light aroma of mesquite grilling with a touch of something else, not quite distinguishable, made everyone's mouth water with anticipation.

The party was planned for seven p.m., but Sandy had to catch a flight out from BWI to Newport, Rhode Island, so Mari-Rae moved up the time to accommodate her. "Thanks," said Sandy. "Not many people would rearrange their own going-away party to fit the time schedule for an out-of-town friend."

"Isn't that what friends do?" Mari-Rae asked.

They perused the menu after ordering half-pitchers of margaritas and mojitos. They were almost too pretty to drink—almost.

"What are you having, Mari-Rae?" Dave asked. They all chuckled, knowing what was coming.

The server arrived, stoically dressed in a high-collared black tunic with a casual smile. Perfect combination. He knew how to work his audience. He explained the specials. "Any questions?" Oh, no, now he did it.

Mari-Rae looked at him and smiled. "The Salmon Salad—what all is in it?"

He went on to explain all the components of the salad exactly as they were listed on the menu.

"But the baby lettuce, is it fresh?" Mari-Rae frowned.

"Yes, ma'am, it was brought in fresh this afternoon."

"And the tomatoes? Are they hot-house raised or natural?"

"I'll check on that for you," the server's smile was not quite as broad.

"Can you put the onions and the peppers on the side?"

"Yes, ma'am."

"What all is in your balsamic vinaigrette?"

"Ma'am?"

Jim had to intercede. "Mari-Rae, give him a break. Just order something."

Everyone laughed, even Mari-Rae.

"Okay, I'll have the Salmon Salad. But I'd like my onions and peppers on the side, and put the dressing on the side, too. And not too much. I never like very much. Oh, and can I substitute the oranges for guava?"

"Mari-Rae, do you want to go back there and make your own salad?" Sandy laughed.

At the end of the evening, everyone ended up outside of Mari-Rae's condo. Her sister, Christina, asked, then almost begged, Mari-Rae to stay with her that night. She refused, saying it was easier to stay at her friend's place right above hers. Mari-Rae turned to say goodbye to her sister. Christina told her to call when she got to California and they exchanged a quick hug.

Mari-Rae held her sister at arms-length. "Ah, T, you can do better than that."

They embraced in a big bear hug.

On Monday, the truck arrived to take her things. She spent a few hours wiping down the condo. She would miss this place. She'd miss all of her good friends. But like everyone else, they wouldn't be forgotten. She had always stayed in touch with her friends, no matter where life took her. This wouldn't be any different. Ahead was the end of the rainbow, the pot of gold–not in a financial sense, but in what she coveted most. Her dream was within her grasp.

9 Why Do Some Days Have to Be So Hard?

"When last seen, Mari-Rae was headed towards her dream."...Mike Sharples, Iowa State Coach

Mari-Rae didn't need an alarm or coffee to be up and peeking out of her friend's upscale D.C. condo before dawn on this beautiful Tuesday Indian summer day. Not just up, but practically vibrating excitement. It was here. Now! The beginning of a new life, *the life* she had dreamed about since she was ten years old. She paused for a moment in the pre-dawn hour and remembered how it all began.

The year was 1976 and she was ten-years-old. On the small television in her family room, Nadia Comãneci scored a perfect ten on the uneven bars. It was the Summer Olympics in Montreal. She vowed that someday, she, Mari-Rae Sopper, would be a professional gymnast. That vision of Nadia, as sharp and vivid as when she first saw it, had been set on auto-play in her mind every day since, taunting her to make her dream come true. And now, it was.

Her new job as head women's gymnastics coach at the University of California Santa Barbara was waiting for her. Never mind that she was taking a seventy percent cut in pay from her current position as a D.C. attorney.

Never mind that they said it was only a one-year position and that the program was being cut at the end of that year. That's what they thought. She had a plan. She *always* had a plan. For UCSB, there would be fund raisers, alumni and booster participation, lots of publicity. She would save the program. It was a given. Anyone who knew Mari-Rae would agree.

She left a voice message for her friend, Jim Bailey, that she'd be ready in half-an-hour. Should she give a last call to her mother? No, she was probably getting ready to head out for a real estate listing appointment. One of the many things Mari-Rae had learned from her mother was perseverance.

She ran down the stairs to her own empty condo. She stepped through the door, a jumble of emotions fluttering her rapidly beating heart: sadness over leaving so many wonderful friends, jubilation about her new position.

"Seriously, Sammy?" She pinched her nose. The hardwood floors were peppered with piles of watery cat feces. "What was wrong with your litter box?" Ah, it was full, too. The medication from the vet was supposed to calm him down for the flight. Wrong. And they never mentioned this unsavory side-effect.

Her feline companion responded by a leap straight into the air from his perch on the spiral staircase, a virtual orange-and-white-striped rocket, that took off across the empty room at a speed that would have made Coach Petrillo proud. Then he slid into the wall—*thud!*

Mari-Rae laughed and shook her head. "Better get your running out of your system now. You'll be stuck in that carrier on the plane for several hours."

Things to do rushed through her head. Shower, check. Light make-up, check. She donned a simple A-line skirt and a button down sweater. It was always chilly on planes and she was always cold. She surveyed herself in the mirror. An even hundred brush strokes. Her dark blond hair shone like the smile on her face. She slipped on a pair of simple flats; easier to maneuver through the airport concourse.

Did she have all of the information on the team in her bag? Check. She'd go over them again on the flight. Not that she didn't already know every team member by name, their statistics, and where they excelled. She had always had the uncanny ability to remember names and scores and details like a flash drive in her head. Ryann was going to be great on beam. Erika only needed some good choreography to win competitions on floor. She loved each and every one of them already.

Jim arrived on time. He beeped the horn. *How did she always manage to get me to drive her to the airport?* Next time he would tell her, "Us city-folk take a taxi." He waited thirty minutes and finally let himself into her condo. Mari-Rae was still running around, ass on fire. What else was new?

He lifted her red backpack to carry to his car. "Ugh," he groaned. "What do you have in here, rocks?" If it made it on as a carry-on, it would be a miracle.

"What?" Mari-Rae looked up from her hands and knees on the hardwood floor. "That's my purse. Can you give me a hand here?" Mari-Rae waved a frantic hand toward the paper towels.

"If I weren't such a good friend…" Jim started as he knelt over a pile, his nose wrinkled from the God-awful smell.

"I know, I know," said Mari Rae as she finished up. "What do you think, Sammy? Are you ready?"

The ride through the Virginia countryside to Dulles Airport was beautiful. If Mari-Rae noticed it, she didn't say. For forty-five minutes, she expounded on the qualities of her new team, how she was going to save the program. This time, this move, would be perfect. Her dream was finally in her grasp.

Jim dropped her off at the curb for departing flights to American Airlines. She hoisted the red backpack over the shoulder of her five-foot-two frame as he unloaded the rest of her luggage and the kitty crate. Life was going to be different without Jim around. She'd miss him. Of course there was still email and phone. They'd talk all the time, she assured herself. They hugged.

"Oh, I don't have any ones. Help me out?" she laughed. *So, shoot me,* she thought. Small details like that didn't make it into her computer brain. They didn't register high on the "needs" list.

Jim shook his head, dug into his wallet and handed over his only ones to tip the luggage handler. "Call me when you get to Santa Barbara," he said.

Of course. He was one of her closest friends.

She waved as he honked and drove away. She looked up at the perfectly blue sky, not a cloud in site. Whew. This was it. Her new life. She remembered the title of the last group email she had sent to all of her family and friends, *New Job, New City, New State, New Life.* If joy was a drink, hers would be an orange Fizzy, like the sugary tablet she dropped into water as a child.

At airport security, she let Sammy out to get some air before the flight and placed the kitty crate on the conveyor belt to go through the scanner. He clung to her like an infant on his mother's shoulder, digging his back claws into her chest. Her eyes began to water from too much fur close to her face. Did she remember her allergy medicine? Yes, of course.

Okay. So maybe letting Sammy out of the cage wasn't one of her best decisions.

She started to walk through the scanner with Sammy on her shoulder.

"Ma'am," a security guard stopped her. "You'll have to put the cat in the carrier, while it goes through the scanner.

Getting him back into the carrier was a war of the wills. Once she pried him from her shoulder, his paws clung to the outside of the cage door, spread-eagled, Felix-the-Cat-like. Two security guards had to assist in winning over Sammy's determination to stay out of that crate. She made her way back to the front of the line and walked through the scanner alone.

Two Middle-Eastern men stood stoically behind her in line. She glanced up at them and profusely apologized for Sammy's rude behavior. They nodded without speaking.

The alarms went off. Mari-Rae and the two gentlemen behind her were pulled aside where the security guard waved a wand over them and finally allowed them to go to the gate. The rest of the passengers went straight through.

All cleared, she picked up Sammy in the carrier and her backpack and asked for directions to the gate. The two Middle-Eastern gentlemen followed her to the same gate.

Finally, at 7:50 a.m., she was settled in her seat, American Airlines Flight 77, Dulles International to LAX, Los Angeles, California. Her seatbelt was on. The stack of papers about "her girls" tucked in the magazine compartment in front of her waiting for her review. Mari-

Rae looked around at the half-empty plane. Her aisle seat was perfect for introducing herself to the fellow passengers across the aisle and in the seat next to hers. "Where are you headed? Wasn't life wonderful?"

At 8:20 a.m., the flight took off on time from runway 30, Dulles International Airport.

8:31:23— Air traffic control from Dulles walked the plane through the climb to flight level two-niner - zero.

8:31:30— Pilot American Airlines 77: "Two-niner-zero American 77."

8:50:48— Indianapolis Control, Henderson Sector Radar: "American 77 cleared direct Falmouth."

8:50:51— Pilot American Airlines 77: "Direct Falmouth American 77. Thank you."

8:56:32— Indianapolis Control, Henderson Sector Radar: "American 77."

8:56:46— Indianapolis Control, Henderson Sector Radar: "American 77."

8:56:53— Indianapolis Control, Henderson Sector Radar: "American 77, American 77. Radio check. How you read?"

8:57:12— Indianapolis Control, Henderson Sector Radar: "American 77, American 77. Radio check. How you read?"

8:58: 30— American Air Lines (central): "Who you trying to get a hold of?"

8:58:33— Indianapolis Control, Henderson Sector Radar: "American 77."

8:58:36— Indianapolis Control, Henderson Sector Radar: "Point to seven, we were talking to him and all of a sudden it just uh . . ."

8:58:38— American Air Lines: "O.K., all right, we'll get a hold of him for ya."

8:58:5— Indianapolis Control, Henderson Sector Radar: "American 77, American 77. Radio check. How do you read?"

9:00:33— Pilot American Airlines 2493: "Yeah, we sent a message to dispatch to have him come up on twenty-twenty-seven. Is that what you want them to do?"

9:00:41— Indianapolis Control, Henderson Sector Radar: "Yeah. We had 'em on west side of our airspace and they went into coast and ah don't have a track on 'em and now he's not talking to me so we don't know exactly what happened to him. We're trying to get a hold of him. We also contacted your company. So thanks for the help."

9:10:34— Indianapolis Control, Henderson Sector Radar: "All right. This is Henderson. There was an American eleven departed off of New York going to L.A. Got hijacked. American 77 departed off of Dulles is going to L.A. Dispatch doesn't know where he's at and confirmed that two airplanes have been, uh, they crashed into, uh, the World Trade Center in New York. So as far as American 77, we don't know where he is.[14]"

The plane never arrived at its destination. Hijacked by *Al Qaeda* terrorists, they carried out the joint plan that also crashed the two planes into the World Trade Center in New York City and another that was thwarted by passengers into a field in Pennsylvania.

At 9:37 a.m., Tuesday, September 11, 2001, American Airlines Flight 77 crashed into the Pentagon, killing all on board; sixty-four souls including the five

---

[14] partial transcript form American Airlines Flight 77 to Air Traffic Control

hijackers and one cat—plus one hundred twenty-five people in the building. Altogether, two thousand nine hundred ninety-six souls were lost that day.

What were those last moments like from the last contact with the pilot at 8:50 until 9:37? Forty-seven minutes. What did she think about? Her friend, Sandy, thought she would have been more concerned about the cat than her own welfare.

Mari-Rae's sister, Lynn, said, "I can see her now, standing up and screaming, 'What do you mean, hijacked? You have no right.'"

Her mother said, "With Mari-Rae on board, well, God help those hijackers."

Mike Sharples, Mari-Rae's Iowa State coach, was quoted at the Memorial Service. "When last seen, Mari-Rae was headed for her dream."

It was all within her grasp. If Mari-Rae could speak to you today, she would have one message.

"Reach for Your Dreams."

10   Reflections and Aspirations

"Mari-Rae was full of fire and spark. That was a little nod from her to us that she will continue to keep us on our toes."   Jennifer Rudy Bannon

Six days later, on Sunday, September 17, 2001, the UCSB men's and women's gymnastics teams and the UCSB chancellor gathered at Jennifer Rudy's apartment in Isla Vista just off of the UCSB campus—where just six days before, the girls were to meet their new coach for the first time. It was going to be a "meet-the-team barbecue," said UCSB junior Cara Simkins in a Sports Illustrated interview. By then, they already felt they knew her. Lesley Ross, a sophomore, told the reporter, "She had an awesome attitude and was so in-love with the sport. She was getting us all pumped up to come back." Silently, they made a single file across the street to an empty grassy lot. Standing at the edge of a ragged cliff, they watched a beautiful sunset kiss the Pacific Ocean in an array of color. They lit candles and placed them on a cloth covered table and spoke of their coach, the inspiration she instilled in them, the burning desire to continue on without her. She was still their coach.

They blew out the candles and headed back across the street to Jennifer's apartment to continue to commemorate Mari-Rae. Sometime later, Jennifer noticed a bright light and saw flames coming from across the street. Jennifer and Mirchea, the men's gymnastics coach, ran across the street frantically smothering the fire. "I couldn't help but laugh," said Jennifer. "Mari-Rae was full of fire and spark. That was a little nod from her to us that she will continue to keep us on our toes."

In Palatine, Illinois, another thousand people gathered earlier in the day, in the gymnasium of Fremd High School. Mari-Rae's high school photo as she balanced on the beam reached into the crowd from the podium.

Mari-Rae's sister, Lynn Sopper Segovia, said, "It is comforting to know Mari-Rae accomplished so much with her life. It's not like we think, she didn't have a chance to live. She was at a high point in her life. A lot of people never reach those high points. That makes it a little easier."

"It's just like her to go down this way and be a part of history," said Marion, her mother, to Jamie Sotonoff and Shruti Danté, staff writers of the Daily Herald in Arlington Heights, Illinois.

Friends, teammates, and colleagues gave their eulogies, through tears and laughter, they recalled the joy of having Mari-Rae Sopper as a part of their lives. Most echoed her mantra. Many pledged to live better lives, be a little kinder to others, a little more forgiving, to go that extra mile for their fellow gymnast, family member, or friend.

Mari-Rae's message was clear. "Reach for your dreams." No matter how distant they seem, no matter the obstacles to overcome, never give up on your dream. Hers was within her grasp on September 11, 2001.

Perhaps the best way to convey Mari-Rae's strongest beliefs is to allow her friends to state their observations: This is how some of family and friends remember Mari-Rae:

"Mari-Rae is an unrelenting force, hungry for excellence . . . I know last Tuesday she entered heaven and she went in full force."…Mike Sharples, Mari-Rae's Gymnastics Coach at Iowa State University (from the memorial service).

"Mari-Rae Sopper did not live in vain and she did not die in vain."

"Passionate, bright, enthusiastic, obvious perfectionist, generous, determined, disciplined, courageous, tolerant, unique, beautiful, talented, trusting, non-judgmental, and full of ideas."

"Mari-Rae was passionate about many things: family, politics, current events, women's rights, friends, and of course, gymnastics. She cherished her relationships."   Laurie Rischer Castillo

"Mari-Rae's greatest qualities were undying conviction and belief in doing the right thing even though it may not be popular or mainstream."

"She taught all of us the meaning of the word determination!"   Sandy Oldham

11   From the Mari-Rae Memorial Website - www.mari-rae.net

Whenever Mari-Rae Sopper did something, she did it in a big way, with long-lasting effects. She will be remembered for her loyalty, strong values, excellent work ethic, and spirit for life. We love her very much and wish her the best, wherever her spirit may be.

"I remember her zeal for gymnastics and genuine love of the sport. I remember her tenderness and romantic grace. I remember her determination, diligence, and talent. I remember her good-natured concern for others. I remember her honesty and humility."   Shaun Hoffmeyer

"We were teammates on the William Fremd H.S. gymnastics team and I remember her tremendous passion! I am so proud to learn of the life she went on to live after high school."   Christel Goins Brady

"I was a senior at Iowa State when Mari-Rae arrived on the scene as a freshman. What a little dynamo! She had the steely determination of someone way beyond her years. As an upper classman, I should have been the one setting an example for her, but it was the other way around..." Deb (Diskerud) Hatanpa

Pentagon (October 12, 2001)
Secretary of Defense Donald Rumsfeld hosted a Department of Defense Memorial Service on the Pentagon's Parade Field, where more than twenty

thousand invited guests included the family members of those who died.

"We are gathered here to remember, to console, and to pray," said Rumsfeld. "We remember them as heroes, and we are right to do so."

President George W. Bush delivered the keynote address. His participation was expected, but not confirmed until invitees were seated and received the service program indicating the President's attendance. His remarks included:

"One life touches so many others. One death can leave sorrow that seems almost unbearable. But to all of you who lost someone here, I want to say: You are not alone. The American people will never forget the cruelty that was done here, and in New York, and in the sky over Pennsylvania.

"We will never forget all the innocent people killed by the hatred of a few. We know the loneliness you feel in your loss. The entire nation shares in your sadness. And we pray for you and your loved ones. And we will always honor their memory."

Al and Tipper Gore: "Mari-Rae's true devotion to the democracy that is the cornerstone of our nation first brought her to our lives. We will always be grateful for her tireless work in Pennsylvania during the 2000 election. She kept the values of our country close to her heart. She was a great presence with her energy and love of life. Know that there are countless people who hold Mari-Rae in the highest esteem."

Mari-Rae's obsession with even numbers haunts her today.

She died at 9:37 a.m.
on 9/11/01
on Flight AA77
at the age of 35.
She is interned at Arlington Cemetery in the Columbarium Niche Wall
Section M3
Stack 11
Niche 1
Court 5.

This book has 11 chapters.

She would not like these numbers at all.

Part of her is also under the Memorial Stone for all Pentagon and AA77 victims at Arlington Cemetery because more of her remains were found after her cremation and her remains being placed in the Columbarium. The family was allowed to place items that held special memories in the wall next to her urn holding her remains. Her mother, Marion, included a couple of plaques she was awarded as a child that said things like "most improved" and "hardest working." Her sister, Christina, put an autographed picture of George Stephanopoulos.

Rest in peace, Mari-Rae.

About the Author

Joanne Simon Tailele, originally from Youngstown, Ohio, wrote her first short story at the age of ten in blue colored pencil. For most of her life, she wrote personal essays and poems, for her family and friends, but mostly for herself.

In 2010, with her family grown, she took on the NANOWRIMO Challenge to write a novel in thirty days. Upon completing the assignment, she spent the next two and half years editing the piece. In 2012, *Accident* was ready for publication. Her second novel, ***Town Without Mercy*** launched in 2013. In 2015, a tenth grandchild and her first children's book, ***What is Family?*** was born.

Her books are available in print and e-book through Amazon.com, Barnesand Noble.com and on her website at **http://www.joannetailele.com**

She is an independent author and free-lance writer for Jacobs Writing Consultants,LLC. When not writing, she enjoys golf and the beach in sunny Florida in her home on Marco Island.

If you enjoyed ***Within Her Grasp***, please leave a review on Goodreads.com, Amazon.com or her Facebook Author page.   Thank you.

Made in the USA
Charleston, SC
19 June 2015